CREATI - WITTY

UNFOLDING THE SECRET FORMULAS OF A CREATIVE TEACHER

ARUN DIVAKARAN

Creati-Witty
1st Edition

Publication Date: August 2022
Price: ₹ 340 $ 6.0
ISBN: *978-93-95673-13-6*
Published by:
Adhyyan Books
Office No. 125,
Opposite Vivanta by Taj,
DDA SFS. Pocket-1, Dwarka,
Sec-22, New Delhi-110077
Website: http://adhyyanbooks.com
E-mail: contact@adhyyanbooks.com

Printed at: Repro Printers, Delhi

CONTENTS

AUTHOR'S NOTE

This book is dedicated to all the educators in the world who have shared their experiences and provided me the guidance that contributed to my personal and professional growth. All the efforts and hard work you invested to bring out the best in us can never be repaid in mere words. My sincere gratitude to you for the selfless and sacrificial contributions in the field of education. I truly appreciate you and the time you spent helping me in many occasions.

The world needs teachers who can inspire students rather than those who bombard with information. It is no secret that the academic landscape is littered with misconceptions about what it means to be a teacher. The world of academia is rife with talk of grades, competition, and pressure. Understanding the various patterns of teaching took me on a journey of learning more about knowing the background of teachers, their mindset, their limitations and challenges and experimented how adding some simple creative flavors in their teaching routine can make a big difference in the way they impart the lessons not just from the academic standpoint but from the life as well.

This book is by no means prescriptive, rather an eye opener to help you transform from your current self. I firmly believe that the real change comes from the inside out.

It is my journey to understand and closely observe the pedagogy of teaching and share the game changing practices that shapes up teachers in preparing the students of tomorrow. Entire book is structured in developing the framework disciplines and tools for creating continuous renewal in teaching community. The creative teaching techniques mentioned in this book, when applied consistently and effectively will create paradigm shift in the way education is imparted. This can leave a legacy behind!

Despite I have put all my efforts to keep this book error free, I ask your forgiveness and take full responsibility for any error you find, for I am still learning and solicit your feedback to my email listed below if there happen to be any.

If in any way, I can assist you in this endeavor, or if you would like to engage in a creative teaching workshop, please write a note to arun.divakaran@hotmail.com. Alternatively, my latest workshops and programs are announced in my digital portfolio, www.impactmaker.in

We can only feel grateful for having a teacher like you!

INTRODUCTION

We are living in the greatest of times where industry is being revolutionized with rapid technology advancements every minute of the day. Artificial intelligence and related technologies are influencing almost every sector including the education field. Machines are being trained to learn and have started to play the role of teachers. In this technology dominant world, anything that is found repetitive is the first candidate for automation and that is quite applicable in the field of education as well. This can be seen as one salient example where the most educated are being made redundant by technology. This thought should enable teachers to go creative in their approaches as we prepare our students to face the future of uncertainty.

We are all aware of the fact that the current design of education reflects the era in which it was originally developed. Industrial revolution was just begun and the need of that hour was to create a work-force that could simply listen to instructions and faithfully execute repetitive work without asking questions. The foundation of our system was originally based on rote learning. We have a certification committee or the education board who fixes a curriculum and the books are published and released in the market accordingly, teachers rushes through the contents of the book and train the students to recall all the information in the book. Then we have the assessment which is measured on ability of the student to actually reproduce what is in the book. Ironically, we are still continuing with the same pedagogy and graduating children from this type of system is surely a recipe for disaster in the present digital era. The time has come to reconsider our approach to teaching and graduate students from this type of system in the digital age. The choice is simple: either sit and blame the system and do nothing or get up, upskill, adapt to the change, and contribute to a system that will help us create a better world.

We cannot wait for a complete reform of national policies around the structure and curriculum of the present educational system as that is not in our control. What we are in control of is the way we adapt to this revolution and inculcate the mindset of explorative Learning and enable multitude of skills beyond academics such as Problem solving, critical thinking, decision making, values, team-work and social skills. Such transformational changes will be possible only if all the key players in a child's life i.e. parents, teachers, educational institutions together provide them a stimulating environment with ample exposure to platforms that nurtures these essential life skills. These will not only make them confident individuals who contribute to the society but will empower them to stay ahead of the smart machines and be future ready.

Teachers are hardwired to prepare students to succeed, but are not trained to help them in handling failures. Failure is a part of life and very often a crucial step to success and learning from them is more significant.

Teachers must refine their teaching process to allow children to think and act differently. They must connect with each child and treat her or him according to her or his needs. They must also be learners as well as teachers in order to do so. The process of studying should be a pleasurable one that encourages original thinking and nurtures the child's curiosity. Grading children based on their ability to memorize content should no longer be performed. They must draw on student's sources of knowledge in order to match the student's access. With the technology we have at our disposal, it is more easily accomplished. The more professional you become on the inside, the more likely your students will take an interest in what you have to share. It's a process of self-improvement that will not only make you a more productive member of society, but it will also make you a more inspiring teacher. It's not something that takes place overnight and it doesn't happen with a click of a button. In order for teachers to prepare students for the future, they must first think outside the box, in other words, teach outside the box, which is the primary objective of this book.

The famous American Actor Will Smith said

"You don't set out to build a wall. You don't say 'I'm going to build the biggest, greatest wall that's ever been built.' You don't start there. You say, 'I'm going to lay this brick as perfectly as a brick can be laid.' You do that every single day. And soon you have a wall."

As you traverse through my book, you will find many such bricks that will help you to build the perfect wall. I would say "The wall of teaching excellence".

OVERVIEW OF THE CONTENTS

In this new book titled "Creati-Witty" I would like to show how you can create joyful classroom community just using some simple interesting techniques with a transformative change in the mindset of the teacher that ultimately creates a lasting impact on the students that helps them build a sense of purpose and autonomy to take ownership of their life.

It follows that there is really no logical order to the book. As you can imagine, creative teaching cannot be reduced to a set of mere sequential procedures or steps. This is not meant for only teachers, it is meant for anyone who directly or indirectly touch other's lives by virtue of the role you play. A Coach, Mentor, Teacher, Child Psychologist, Education Management, Leaders, Parents etc. There is no end to the list.

I hope that you find this book stimulating and enjoyable as well as constructive. May it uplift you forward on your journey as a creative teacher. Among other things, these chapters will help you to develop deep understanding of the current self as a teacher, retrospection of your journey so far, understanding of the future readiness skills needed, the generation of students and their thinking levels, the best practices to engage students, improve the overall learning outcome, enlarge your parameters of vision, learn to experiment and build on ideas, increase your power of resilience to deal with uncertainties, learn to taking calculated risks, mindfulness with a creative attitude etc.

Each chapter has one core idea. Depending on its kind, I then briefly develop and illustrate it with examples graphically so as to help you understand and blend it in your belief system.

The book consists of nine chapters. Chapter one provides a brief history of my journey into teaching and the struggles I went through during my learning process. Every reader may be able to relate himself/herself in those situations especially if you did you schooling during the 90s.

Chapter Two highlights the differences between being a teaching graduate vs being a teacher and challenges you the question on why you want to be a teacher? What drove you into this profession? How learning and teaching are coupled together? What is the mindset shift required for an outcome driven learning? I have shared my own experiences as a student and how different styles of teachers have impacted both positively and negatively in my life.

Chapter Three helps you assess your current creative teaching skill through a well-researched psychometric framework. It identifies your current gaps in teaching and prepares you to start the journey of transformation. After discussing with several teachers and my personal experiences, I have carved out certain teaching styles and approaches that paves the way for teaching in a creative manner. It is a scoring system with report. You must be 100% honest with yourself when taking up the psychometric exercise. There is no one to judge you, but yourself.

Chapter Four kick starts your transformation journey as a future ready teacher. It reflects the mental cob-webs of the current day teacher and helps you to deal with them. It also highlights the differences of a fixed and growth mindset and takes you through rigorous six practical steps to become a future ready teacher. The chapter then highlights the E.G.O factor in teachers and how it plays as a barrier in their learning journey. It addresses an important need of today which is to teach students not only the ways to succeed but also ways to handle failures.

Finally, this chapter emphasizes the need to teach mantras to stay happy.

Chapter Five discusses about the impact created by the pandemic across the globe for both the teaching community and the learners. It depicts the huge rise in the role of technology in the field of education and how both teachers and students need to upskill themselves in dealing with the online gadgets and the mindset shifts that doesn't compromise on the emotional and mental health.

Chapter Six throws light on the different generation of students and their shift in thinking patterns and how teachers need to prepare themselves to deal with the post millennial students (Gen-Z).

Chapter Seven is all about the best practices to help students transform as impact makers. It traverses through all authentic activities right from getting to know your student, performing classroom aerobics, collaborative learning practices, classroom edutainment and using techniques that ignites interest in the subject for a joyful learning.

Chapter Eight shares short inspiring stories about teachers that stimulates one's imagination and potentially change the way the teacher look at events in his/her routine.

Chapter Nine shares you several newspaper/magazine articles on teaching that I collected over a period of time.

ACKNOWLEDGMENTS

I have greatly enjoyed sharing my experience, knowledge and experiments about "Creative Teaching" to a wide range of teachers. As I have taught on such topics in a wide variety of platforms including College & School premises, Online webinars and Conferences, they wished to understand how I had managed to capture the imagination and attention of various students with so much of energy and enthusiasm, how I inspired so many teaching staff to act, and what teaching best practices and principles assisted me as a teaching coach. This publication will answer all these queries, providing a valuable look at one of the most innovative teaching methods in recent years.

It is a particular pleasure to write this book, because it is about creativity in teaching and that is what humans are meant for. What differentiates between Man and Machine is in the ability of the former to think creatively. Machines perform better than humans in doing repeated tasks efficiently. To make the world a better place, both needs to co-exist. Just as I enjoyed evangelizing the concept of creative teaching, I also enjoyed writing this book immensely, and I owe a special thank you to the many people who supported me throughout the writing process.

I would like to thank my wife, who lights my life each day and encouraged me to go above and beyond. A special thanks to my dad whom I consider as the world's best, who has till date never compared me with anyone and gave me enough freedom during my school and college days to explore my dreams without being judged, My loving mom who showed me the right path of life, My uncle from whom I learnt to do things in life without expecting anything in return, My grandpa who is not with me today but I am sure he will be feeling proud and showering his blessings from the above, I feel it was his mentorship that awakened the teacher coach in me. I am connected to him through the letters he wrote to me during my childhood, then my compassionate paternal grandma whom I miss, my maternal grandma from whom I just love to be scolded even this day, my sister who has stood by me in tough times and my little ones who were very cooperative during the days of my writing. A heartful of love to my cousins, uncles, aunts, my friends and, obviously, my peers – the teachers, who are already great in their profession, yet strive to get even better. They have taught me far more than I have ever taught them.

Finally, nothing can happen without the blessings from the force above. A bow to the Almighty with full of gratitude. I also want to thank you as the reader who has chosen my book to bring changes in your mode of teaching.

Happy Learning!

1

"TEACHING IS HARD; IT'S HARDER IF YOU'RE NOT CREATIVE."

Why I wanted to write this book – The STORY Behind.

The purpose of writing a book about creative teaching is to counter the prevailing belief that teaching is a risk free and safest job in the market and that one can easily generate income for their livelihood if he/she has a graduate in the teaching field.

As a teacher coach, I realize that the school system isn't perfect in terms of teaching or developing the habits of great learning in our student community. Based on my routine interaction with many teaching professionals, I realized that most often than not, these educational institutions and their teaching staff are too much bound up in the rat-race routine that includes repetitive paperwork, finishing up portions, following textbook guidelines, preparing for audits etc. As a result, their collective focus around student community narrows down to the level of just meeting national standards, measuring their quality by means of grades, following unrealistic checklists etc. The teaching thought process thus becomes stagnant and their typical daily routine gets heavily mechanical to be perceived as a teaching machine. This experience can make learning later in life more of a struggle. If we can reframe that thinking and repurpose their existence where learning would mean going creative and experimenting newer ideas, it suddenly becomes more attractive, interesting and engaging.

Of my many interactions with students, fellow teachers and the system resources as whole, I learned a lot on what is lacking in the today's educational eco system. With so many private institutions, there is huge demand for teachers. However, most of the times, the primary motto of these institutions is to build their business. The values are measured in terms of profits and not by the quality of education and learning effectiveness. As a result, teachers are treated as laborers where they sign a bond with the hiring institution for a specific period of time with a fixed salary. Under these circumstances, one can imagine how their output is going to be. Over a period of time, their job gets too monotonous and they get into a belief for themselves that they are doing the job for the sake of it. This is the harsh reality of many of today's teachers. This book is intended to uplift the morale of the teachers who feel stuck in their routine jobs and how they can create a transformative path for themselves.

The main impetus for the writing of this book comes from the fact that we are all passionately committed to a move away from the obsession with education being perceived as merely a means to an end and schools valued according to their test and examination results. We, like many others in education, have a huge desire to see learning as central to the process of schooling. As mature adults, we have become more or less excited by our own learning as time passes and have often felt keenly the sense of waste when we hear young people speak of their schooling as boring and who are impatient for it to finish. The fault in most cases is not of theirs. Although we have ideals, we are also pragmatists who believe that for the people in our schools the future starts now. Actions have to be taken and taken soon. The case studies in this book show just how many of our schools share such beliefs and are already doing things to make their students' and staff's experiences meaningful, relevant and exciting. There are also many schools where people would like to make changes but are not sure how to begin or lack confidence to do so. There are also schools where initiatives have been started, only for them to ponder after a while, causing a loss of faith in the change process itself.

This book attempts to take a whole school view of approaches to making learning central, so that staffing and structures, external links and resources, are all dealt in ways with which learning schools can evolve. We believe that without examining every aspect of school activity, an emphasis on learning will remain an 'add-on'. This of course does not mean everything can be attempted at once!. School leaders and managers know that what you do next depends on what you are doing now, particularly in regard to learning and teaching. Nearly all the chapters therefore include suggestions for practical and specific steps that you may wish to consider as the next step for your school. We have set out a model for change within which these steps can be taken. We have to stop pretending to be someone we are not and striving for things that are not aligned with our true values. This will free us to pursue our own unique purpose. A Life built on deep self-awareness will always lead to greater fulfillment and success.

The world is filled with Doctors, Engineers, Artists, Writers, Scientists, Laborer's, Designers, Marketers, Technologists, Drivers, Chefs, Sports Personalities and numerous other professions.

Isn't it great to know that behind all these professions, there is always a TEACHER who has had a major impact on their development in some way. That is what makes teaching such a divine thing. They are creators of every other professions and hence in Indian culture they are treated as messengers of God.

I consider 3 major services that are divine and selfless in naturc,

1. The Doctors & Nurses.
2. The Military & Police
3. Teachers & Gurus

Of the three listed above, the #3 gets the least attention and recognition in the world today which is the sad state of affair.

This is what makes the country progress. You must have heard of dignity of labor; every job has dignity and the person doing it also should be dignified.

I was in 12th grade and Physics, Chemistry and Maths have always fascinated me right from my school days. I would like to share the episode of my battle with Physics and how I lost interest in the subject inspite of many lovable concepts in it. As I write the story now, I feel every incident that I faced during the time as fresh as it happened just yesterday.

I was sitting in the one of middle benches and on the first day of my 12th grade enters my Principal introducing the new physics teacher.

There is always some anxiety in the students mind whenever a new teacher is introduced. We too were very excited, obviously quite anxious.

He straight away asked us to open the first chapter even before he introduced himself or asked us to introduce.

He had a little bit of rude looks so with all due respect, we opened the first chapter and were eagerly waiting for him to start the session.

He started reading the lines one by one. Around 20 minutes passed by and there was no eye contact or looking up at us. We were wondering what was going on, my friends on the other end started to play joining-the-dots game (A game played during class room sessions, when things get really boring).

Our classes sessions are held for 45 minutes and he kept on reading the lines till 40 minutes. Most of the others were fully busy doing their own sweet little stuff and I was busy looking at all others.

This went on for many days, weeks and months. There were no signs of engagement with the students. It was a routine affair for the teacher who is quite punctual and enters the class on time and finishes the topic on time. However, his habit of reading the lines of the book never stopped.

As you can by now guess, it took me no time to feel hatred towards the Physics subject. I used to wonder why does teachers have to do this to us. We were all helpless and no one to go to. It was in the middle nineties and that is when I just saw a working computer for the first time.

Physics as a subject is very interesting and I chose to start reading things by myself. We struggled to understand the concepts as this whole internet was a completely unknown phenomena at that time. Hence there were no references we could search anywhere. Luckily there were some tuition centers who offered to provide sessions for a fee.

There were many such instances where I felt, the hatred towards a particular subject need not be with the student but mostly to do with the teachers approach towards it. He might be scholar in the subject and would have got into schools by virtue of his ranks, knowledge and experience. However, what is the point if he is unable to express it in the way that is understood by the students of all cadres. I realized that there are indeed teachers who have opted this profession not by choice but due to the fact that they don't have much choices.

I also have been blessed with some great teachers in my life who were not just teachers but a close mentor.

Realization of my passion in Teaching.

A Teacher plays a great role in shaping us to be better citizens and to be better self. One need to be blessed to have a good teacher in life.

There are several instances in my life where teachers have both been a blessing and a bane for me. Bad teachers gave me lessons to learn what not to do when you are the teacher while all the good teachers lead from the front and taught me what to do as teachers.

Sir Sarvepalli Radhakrishnan

It will be unfair if I don't mention about Sir Sarvepalli Radhakrishnan in a book meant for Teachers or Teaching Parents or Teacher Aspirants.

The world celebrates Teacher's Day on October 15, but in India, this important day is celebrated on September 5, the birthday of Dr. Sarvepalli Radhakrishnan, an academic philosopher and India's second President. He is regarded as One of India's most distinguished twentieth-century scholars of comparative religion and philosophy.

Dedicated to this great man's memory, the occasion is looked forward to by students and teachers alike. It provides an opportunity to take a moment and thank some of the most important people in our lives, the ones who impart knowledge and instruct us.

The great and lasting influence a teacher can have on the student's life is undeniable, and a good teacher is remembered forever.

Dr. Sarvepalli Radhakrishnan staunchly believed in the importance of education and was one of India's celebrated diplomat, politician, scholar and above all, teacher.

Why I love Teachers day? – The IKIGAI moment.

To make September 5 a memorable day, students will don their favorite teacher's cap and literally imitate them. We, Students pose ourselves as teachers and go to various junior classes to handle sessions. The senior grade students would ask us to volunteer to be any teacher of our choice. I opted to be the science teacher as I loved the subject personally. There was a rule that one cannot take up more than one teacher role, however my love to interact with students made me take up other teacher roles bypassing the rule. I requested my class mates to give me their roles without letting the seniors know just to make use of that teaching opportunity. That was my craze to be with students.

I used to long for this day every year since then and the first time I ever went while I was in 8th grade and I was assigned to be the science teacher, Science being my favorite subject.

My First Experience as a Teacher

I came early and skipped the sports classes so as to prepare for the next day session. I was super excited and waited for the next day to dawn fast. I got up early with all excitement unlike other days where I was one of the lazy students and go back to bed once alarm rings. I got ready very fast and cycled fast to school. School was located around 5 kilometers from my home and I used to get goose bumps just by visualizing the upcoming events.

Our schools start as early as 7:30 AM and I rode my cycle fast enough to reach the school and to deliver my first session. It was for 6th grade science. As I entered the class, students (my juniors) greeted me and they too were super excited to see a familiar face in a new role. The classes are for 40 minutes and I started my session with full preparation. The bell rang after the first period and I was hesitating to leave the class as my subject was not complete. Thankfully it was my friend's class and I requested for additional 15 minutes to which he graciously agreed.

15 minutes quickly went by and as I completed my topic and about to leave, the entire students stood up and clapped continuously the sound of which is still heard in my sleep some times.

The entire day went by in this fashion. Towards the end there was a reward and felicitation session for the best teacher enact and never ever I realized that I would be the winner. I was told to have handled 4 classes that was assigned to me on record and that secured top feedback. Infact it was 7 unofficially as I kept borrowing my friend's classes. This experience gave me huge motivation to build myself from there on the lines of teaching.

How to get the maximum value from this book?

Education should not just be about expanding your knowledge and intelligence

It should enable you to take up any job with utmost happiness. It should nourish your physical capacities and health. That is real education. We need everyone in this society, like Autorickshaw drivers, taxi drivers, tailors, business men, cloth merchandise, Hair stylists, delivery boys etc. It is all of these that make this society what it is today.

By pushing aside our normal human emotions to embrace false positivity and pretending we are fine when we are not, we tend to lose the ability to deal with the world as it is and instead fool ourselves into believing it is how we wish it to be. While you are reading these lines, I am sure you would have realized by now that some failure in life is absolutely inevitable, it is impossible to live without failing at something. Our first level of acknowledgement is to accept that failure is an inevitable part of our learning journey, we will realize that the only way to truly fail is by never trying in the first place.

I am approaching the art of creative teaching from a completely different perspective. Instead of focusing on being in charge and telling teachers what to do, I am evoking the focus on their mission and purpose for existence. I recommend that you read through the chapters and answer the reflection questions, either on your own or as part of a discussion with colleagues. Case studies, research information, and personal experiences are provided, along with practical applications for you to apply in your classes.

This book will give you many ideas on how you can capitalize on the positive, and minimize the negative, outcomes of these trends by developing yourself as a skilled and versatile teacher.

2

ARE YOU A TEACHER OR JUST A TEACHING GRADUATE?

If you are just teaching students, that is good enough, but if you can make them think, make them ponder, sensitize them and help them identify their best of abilities, then that is a sign of creative teaching. - Arun Divakaran

During my School days, my dad would come home from work and ask things like, "How was your day today?" or "Which teacher kept you engaged the most today", or "What did you learn from your class today". Most standard response would be "Nothing Much". I used to wonder what he truly meant by those questions. It took nearly 2 decades for me to get the right response to those questions. Today I am confident that if he asks me the same question, I will have lot better and more precise answers.

As a teacher who instills creativity in his teaching style, I would ensure that when parents of my students ask the same questions to their children, they would be gladly be responding on a more positive note.

During my school and college days, I have studied under various teachers and have been exposed to many different teaching styles and methods. I would like to share some of the good and bad experiences from their approach towards me and my fellow students and their overall contributions to the learning habits. Many of the 90s school kids may be able to relate it to their experiences as well.

The Flip side stories

1. English teacher in 8th had a good command in English but was lethargic in finishing the chapters. She was quite vocal, approachable but anger takes a toll on her. Her angry tone would be heard across all the neighboring classes.
2. Maths teacher in 8th was very poor in English and prefers only some students who were good at maths over others. He doesn't even make eye contact with other students whom he felt are not good in the subject.
3. The science teacher had a bad taste in teaching. Her explanations would never make sense. She focused only on the students sitting in the front

rows and never encouraged participation from others. She was quite judgmental about everyone which is a very bad approach.

4. There were teachers who thinks that giving impositions such as making them write something n number of times would fix things. This might have worked in some instances in the past but never take this approach with the Gen-Z students. The concept of imposition needs to be wiped out of the system completely.
5. My Science teacher in 10th asked us to just read the chapter aloud while he doses off. Yes, it was quite gutsy of him! It was a secured government job you see. I hope such instances would be rare in this generation.
6. Discrete Maths teacher in in PG college was quite knowledgeable but was poor in content delivery. Most of the students plays the connect dots game during her class.
7. Geography teacher in 10th was an approachable person but very prompt in starting a class and ending a class, means if he was intending to complete the sentence for e.g. "The study of geography involves knowledge of places understanding of the maps and environment throughout the world" and if the bell rang at the time he was reading the word "Knowledge" he would abruptly end there. He wouldn't even

complete the sentence. Can it be termed as super punctual that you can't even complete the sentence?

8. Social studies teacher kept advising us more than teaching the subject. She kept on advising a lot on every day, during the prayer meeting, while getting caught in the corridor, while recess and lunch breaks. As a result, students stopped taking her seriously and made a mockery out of her.
9. The microprocessor subject teacher in my PG had good body language and a reasonable flow of English but lacked substance. He does not even know what he is teaching and speaking. The folks in the front rows just nods their head to show him that they understood it very well.
10. The Digital Computer Fundamentals teacher in PG had good command on teaching and body language but she happen to be only good in basics. She just could not carry on her command when handling subject in depth. She used that power and command to keep herself from being exposed of this reality.
11. My KV Principal, can never speak few lines of English in the assembly. I don't recollect any good memories of him that encouraged us as students. That clearly tells the fate of the teachers who are reporting to him.
12. My Physics teacher in 12th used to come with the

book titled "ABC of Physics" and kept reading through it without even making eye contact with the students. It was like, if the class was empty, he would still teach the same way.

13. The Hindi teacher in school used to hit the students. Glad that such teachers seldom exist in today's world. Thanks to the social media world as there is fear of being exposed.
14. My 10th grade English teacher had great command in the language. However, she prefers her way of writing essays by every student or benchmarks a particular student's essay which she felt meets her expectation. When we were asked to write an essay on the topic "Library", I had my own views to it. She bluntly rejected it because it was not according to her standards and made everyone in the class to use her words and write.
15. In my very first day in the computer PG course, Me and my friend were sent out of the class just because we did not know to draw a flow chart. Imagine the emotions that we would have gone through. I don't understand what message was she trying to convey. Showing strictness and being arrogant are not the same.

I sometimes used to feel, if there was a time machine, I would like to go back to these days in with my current experience and handle workshops to help these teachers transform their mindset and make them cultivate student centric learning habits.

I would like to share some of the good experiences with teachers too. It is because of such teachers, I got to be what I am today and was able to even get to writing this book.

The Good side stories

1. A Temporary Maths teacher during my 9th was very friendly. She gelled well with students. She held students in loving and caring manner. It was because of her I gained interest in Maths. Gladly she accepted our requests for tuitions because as per the school norms the temporary teacher will be replaced once the permanent one is back. So, me and some of my friends who were on the same boat went for classes separately. Her home was around 6 kilometers from my home. Inspite of the distance, we used to cycle to and from. During 2015 we had a school reunion after 22 years. I was very particular to meet this teacher and my friends obliged and took us there although they were initially hesitant as some of them did not know her much. It took us some time to get the right address but we put all the efforts required to meet her and gladly we were able to meet her.

Everyone then agreed my request to meet her was great. The minimal time we spent was simply joyful. That is the power of a teacher.

2. Our Chemistry teacher in 12th. She was handling classes in another school and we went for special classes in lieu of the board exams. Her politeness and explaining power of the subject was mind blowing. She has profound interest in the subject and hence we loved to listen to her. She made it more interesting for us to better grasp the subject.
3. My Maths professor during college was very compassionate old man. He never referred the books while solving any maths problems. Perhaps that is what I would say experience is. It just kept flowing out of his mind. His problem-solving skills were extraordinary and had immense patience to explain even the basic doubts even when asked n number of times. Once after a cricket tournament, I went to his class as I did not want to miss it and unknowingly showed signs of sleep. The teacher noticed that and very politely requested me to visit his house which was above where he used to handle classes (west Mambalam, Chennai). Upon entering his house, I was surprised to see his wife serving me ginger tea. That gesture moved me a lot.
4. Mothers are always the best teachers no matter what. She can easily blend the life skills with the

academics. Mine was no different case. It was during my middle school days when after the tutoring sessions, she would send me to nearby shop with a grocery list. Here is the lesson. If there are 10 items to buy. She would purposefully give just enough that can manage only 7 items. It was up to me to prioritize things that would not only be helpful for home but also fit within in the budget. I was able to learn, money management, prioritization skills. She would set me the time to be back home as she knows if I meet my friends on the way, I would be spending time with them. This created a time management sense in me. These are just small examples compared to what she has taught me. I am sure all of you will have similar stories to share.

5. The next episode of learning happened to be from a training institute which handled session on engineering physics. The teacher attached every explanation of the subject to some analogy and I just loved that. It became easy for me to absorb the subject. This is where I started to learn to attach analogy if you want to explain any topic better. I have added more thoughts around the usage of analogy in the later part of this book.
6. My Cousin spent his initial days of work at Chennai and stayed with us. I was doing my PG in computer science. It was becoming hard for me

to understand the C++ programming language and the RDBMS concepts. He came up with a simple hands-on fun filled approach to make me understand the concepts in a funny way. He took me to the roots of the topics, added humor and ignited the interest in the subject. I got better at it as days passed and with consistent hands-on practices I was able to master these concepts and soon started handling classes on such topics.

I have listed only few experiences of my student life and what I learned as a teacher. The teachers can make or break the confidence of a child. That is why I took so much of time to and emphasizing the importance of you as a teacher in this world. You may not be the kings but well known for creating king makers. Now let me ask two simple questions to you.

1. Why did you choose or want to choose teaching as your profession? What inspired you to take this role?
2. Are you a teacher with quality who is outcome driven or a mere teacher graduate (with just a qualification) who has come to this position as just another means of generating revenue for your livelihood?

A comparative study on the displays of teachers with different attitudes are shown below. I created two categories. The first category of teacher is a mere graduate in teaching while the second category are teachers with coaching abilities and are more qualitative. The former focusses primarily on output while the latter focusses on outcome. An output driven teacher considers him/herself successful if their students have 100% attendance or attained higher grades in their subjects where-as an outcome driven teacher doesn't go entirely by marks rather tries to evaluate her/his students based on the understanding of the subject. He will reward marks if the students did a practical demonstration of what they learned than memorizing the notes from the text book or reference materials and dump it in the answer sheets. If the students are able to articulate their understanding in any format, either graphical, mind maps, visual or writing it is considered a good learning outcome. The differences in the way of thinking within teacher of different mindsets are represented graphically.

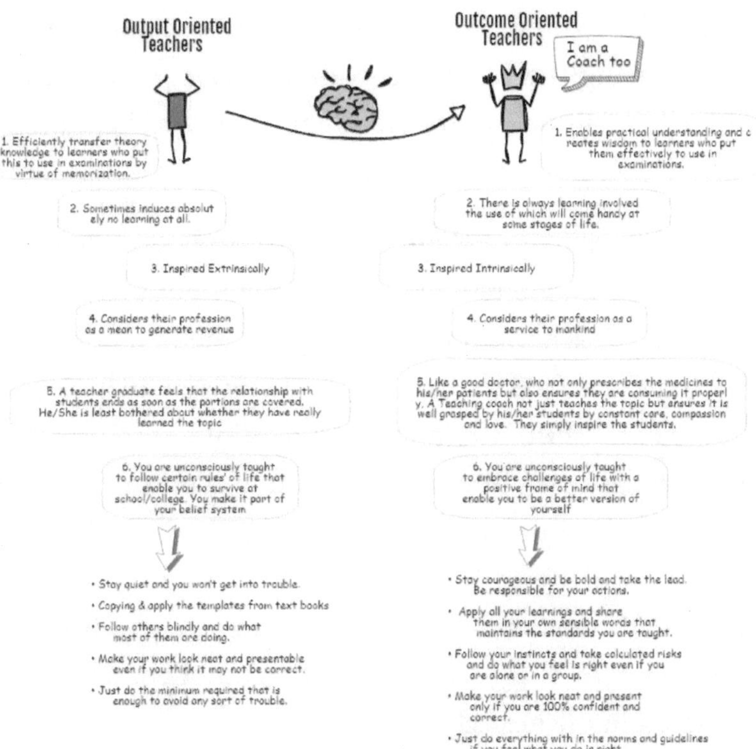

These may appear ironic but the researches have proven that many learners in our schools and colleges just learn the processes that enable them to stay relatively unnoticed. I am sure you would have noticed students who has gone through a whole day without uttering a single word in class. If you closely observe the points that I have shared above, most of the cases, these learners had unconsciously installed the above 'rules' thinking they are true.

So now if you recollect what I mentioned in the opening paragraph of this chapter about the questions that my dad asked after I come from school, I realize now that I was just following the rules that were set by my teacher and that my mention of the familiar two words 'nothing much' was more truthful in that context.

If you are able to relate your approaches in teaching through the above references and if you happen fall into the "Just a Teacher graduate" category, then do not worry. You have a sheer drive to change which is the fundamental shift of mind that is required to move to the coach category. By the time you get a good grasp of my techniques from this book and if applied in the right areas, I assure you would become a master in creative teaching in no time. A deeply researched psychometric assessment to find out the creative quotient in you is discussed in the next chapter.

Let us do a small activity now. You might want to pause here for a moment and follow the steps below.

1. Think absolutely deep and recollect every moment where you learned something without being taught.
2. Open your phone notes app or notepad from your PC.
3. List down all the learning outputs and outcomes that you, as a teacher was responsible for influencing your students till date. Visualize and retrospect how your style of teaching has yielded

the various learning outputs and outcomes within your students. Keep it as honest as you can.

4. Once you are done with typing/writing down your notes, set it aside and get back to your routine. Visit these notes after couple of days or so and read through it as if you are reading it for the first time. This freshens up your perspective and will open up new arenas of your retrospective analysis that you might have missed to capture initially. This will make you realize what you are good at and what you are not. Both of these are a crucial part of our learning experience.
5. We can then make decisions about what to do about them and develop strategies to manage effectively in those areas where you found yourself as not so strong.

3

THE ART OF CREATIVE TEACHING, CHECK YOUR CREATIVE TEACHING QUOTIENT THROUGH ASSESSMENT.

"You can be an extraordinarily creative teacher by just being the best version of yourself"

Creativity and Curiosity goes hand in hand. If you are creative, curiosity kicks in automatically and if you are curious, creativity drives you. Research on curiosity found that kids at the age group of 5 scored 98% on creativity test and the same set of kids took the test at the age of 10, 30% of them scored well and when the same was conducted at the age of 15, 12% of them did well. The irony is only 2% of adults passed the same test. The declining score suggests that one tend to stop being curious as they grow up as they feel there is no gap between what they know and what they wanted to know. We should note that curiosity keeps us young, helps you learn and makes us create solutions to all the problems we come across.

A Teacher plays a very crucial role in igniting curiosity amongst the students. To make that happen the teachers themselves need to be very curious and hone their creative thinking skills before motivating the children. Here is a very interesting question that teachers must ask themselves. What does one mean by creative teaching and how does it differ from the regular methods of teaching. How to Make Creative teaching a habit!

Let us do a small assessment to find out your creativity quotient in teaching. These questions are based on take aways from hundreds of surveys, questionnaire sessions, workshop results conducted with the teaching fraternity. Keep yourself honest in assigning the scores. Remember, this a self-assessment and the first step into creative teaching is to be honest with yourself. We will talk about the improvement methods in our subsequent chapters. You can take as much time as you want but answer each of them with utmost honesty and deep introspection. Remember you chose to read this book as you wanted to improve yourself as a teacher and it is strictly private. So, no need to have the fear of being judged by anyone.

How the psychometric test is designed?

There are 2 parts to the questionnaire. PART-A focusses on your teaching styles, aptitude, personality and socio-emotional skills. PART-B is purely on the teaching attitude. The numeric score card is different for both the parts. The final score is calculated based on the summation both the parts. Since this is an offline version, the score has to be calculated in manual. The online version comes with a graph and auto calculation of the score.

How to take up the psychometric test?

The following assessment scoring system has 5 answers each associated with a number. The answers are "Always", "Most of the times", "Sometimes", "Rarely" and "Never". When doing the test manually, you need to circle the number against each question. For e.g. if you answer is "Most of the times", the value will be 4 and that of "Rarely" will be 2. The score is calculated towards the end of this exercise.

Good Luck! Remember Answer with 100% honesty for best results.

	PART - A Psychometric Assessment for Creativity Teaching Quotient *(Online Assessment can be taken by writing to the author's email id mentioned in the Author's note section)*	5 - Always 4 - Most of the Times 3 - Sometimes 2 - Rarely 1 - Never				
1	I find new ways in handling any repeated topic to my students. (for e.g. when you are handling a session on a same topic to another set of students, you add something new to the topic and not repeat or adopt to same style of teaching that you have already used to)	5	4	3	2	1
2	I explore better ways to engage the students than what is specified in the text book or instructed by the management. (Some teachers go out of their stereotypical methods to explain few things in a way that engages the students better like, role plays, videos, storytelling, visual representations etc.)	5	4	3	2	1
3	I love to read books, blogs, watch videos on self-improvement and explore ways to better engage the student's community.	5	4	3	2	1
4	I am equally approachable by students who are not good at studies and are from other classes/sections/groups/branches of study.	5	4	3	2	1
5	I keep a calm attitude and a positive outlook no matter how stressful a situation is in the institution or outside.	5	4	3	2	1
6	I instill leadership qualities in my students and create every possible opportunity to help them demonstrate their leadership skills be it speeches, debates, thought articulations, school and class responsibilities etc.	5	4	3	2	1

7	I take every opportunity to teach life skills to students in a class even if it's not considered as a scope of my role.	5	4	3	2	1
8	I voluntarily visit other teacher's classes or even other schools with their consensus and try to learn from them.	5	4	3	2	1
9	I use social media to network with teachers from different parts of the globe and be part of regular meet ups regarding better student engagement	5	4	3	2	1
10	When some students deliberately attempt to disturb the discipline of my class by indulging in some sort of mischief, I will try to find out the deeper reasons and help them improve their behavior.	5	4	3	2	1
11	I create a good classroom environment by keeping a lively student-teacher interaction consistently.	5	4	3	2	1
12	If I don't know an answer for a question posted by my student, I have no hesitation is saying "I don't know" but with utmost sincerity, I will research and find the best answer for the student.	5	4	3	2	1
13	I loved to be asked many questions on the subject I handle. It doesn't matter to me if the time allocated to me is exceeded. I am satisfied only if all of their queries are answered. (When I am being asked many questions by the students, I have felt that inviting as it improves my current understanding of the subject and make be better prepared for the subsequent classes)	5	4	3	2	1
14	I believe that Joy/Happiness in the classroom is important for the day to day learning. I love to interject humor into lessons and joke with students. I feel humor makes the entire classroom environment more inviting and engaging.	5	4	3	2	1

15	I think that am approachable by my students irrespective of my mood. I don't let my mood affect the approachability of my students. (e.g. Student conversation: "Hey Science teacher is in bad mood, it is better not to ask any doubts today"	5	4	3	2	1
16	I always feel I have areas of improvement and I would love to upskill myself continuously. In other words, I feel there are better ways to teach something than how I thought today.	5	4	3	2	1
17	I feel that sometimes students know certain things better than me and that they articulate them better than me.	5	4	3	2	1
18	I prefer to have fun in the classroom when body language of students change as they started to feel the topic is getting bored.	5	4	3	2	1
19	I like to keep my classroom ambience high (Elementary classes - Colorful & decorative, Middle & High School - Arts, crafts, Maths & Science project, College - Project works, experiments, student's creative ideas etc.) I ensure that all these activities are exclusively designed, prepared and contributed by each and every student of the class.	5	4	3	2	1
20	I apologize to students if I make any mistake or get late for something that I had promised or even entering the class late.	5	4	3	2	1
21	I am a coach than a mere trainer. I empathize with the students. I think through their minds and try to understand what they are going through and help them to cope with what they are going through.	5	4	3	2	1

22	I feel am an established subject teacher after being in this profession for a relatively longer period. However, I take initiative to handle another subject or topic that is equally of my interest that can help students in the long run.	5	4	3	2	1
23	I like to provide individual attention to my students to the best of my belief and abilities.	5	4	3	2	1
24	I care about the background of my students, such as parent's profession, upbringing environment, their social circle etc.	5	4	3	2	1
25	Say you are a maths teacher and Student A is extremely good in Maths. Would you always benchmark Student A in your class for this subject and keep promoting him on every occasion?	5	4	3	2	1
26	I carry the same energy and enthusiasm as I enter into the class no matter how many times in a day.	5	4	3	2	1
27	When evaluating answer sheets, I look for how much the student has understood the concept and reward him/her accordingly even if it is not exactly worded as per the answer I am looking for.	5	4	3	2	1
28	I treat all parents of my students equally no matter what how influential they are in the society or their profession.	5	4	3	2	1
29	When asking a question to bunch of students, I don't just focus only on the ones raising the hands but also others who don't raise too and encourage them to answer the questions.	5	4	3	2	1
30	I spend additional time with students, discussing non-academic topics and encourage everyone to read news, books, interesting innovations and have healthy debates based on chosen topics. I	5	4	3	2	1

31	I value the back benchers equally as much I value the front runners. I believe that they can do wonders if properly groomed.	5	4	3	2	1
32	I am equally approachable by students who are not good at studies and are from other classes/sections/groups/branches of study.	5	4	3	2	1
33	I believe in "Healthy body for a healthy mind" principle. I encourage and practice a lot of team building mindset, art of communication, sports, yoga and meditation to my students.	5	4	3	2	1
34	I feel I have the right strategies that helps to create rapport and synchronization within in the student community. In other words, I experimented and adopted some best practices that enables healthy student spirit and prevents groupism.	5	4	3	2	1
35	I create a classroom where students are encouraged and inspired to think and articulate their ideas into value added results.	5	4	3	2	1
36	I firmly trust and believe that my students will never talk bad about me because of the way I treat them with respect, care and compassion.	5	4	3	2	1
37	I feel Emotional maturity, integrity, and compassion are more important than training on academic skills and processes.	5	4	3	2	1
38	I feel students of other section/branches approaches me not only for subject doubts but also for socio psychological support and school/college activities consultation.	5	4	3	2	1
39	while you were in charge and in your position of responsibility, do your students come and share their accomplishments and credit you for the support you provided?	5	4	3	2	1

40	I prefer to have a title of "king maker" than being called as a king	5	4	3	2	1
41	I am more inclined to know how much my students have understood the subject than rush to finish up the portions.	5	4	3	2	1
42	When I take leave or vacation, I feel the students miss me a lot. They have expressed the same on various occasions.	5	4	3	2	1
43	I get very excited when students share an interesting idea with me and I do everything possible to make into a reality, even if that means to involve my peers or others from my friend circle.	5	4	3	2	1
44	I get liberal in providing marks for students who are exceptionally talented on any non-academic activity, such as sport, music, art, dance etc.	5	4	3	2	1
45	I keep a good rapport with parents of all of my students and make them feel approachable towards me.	5	4	3	2	1

Now Continue with the PART-B

Please note the scoring point system of the Part-B questions is in the **reversed order**. You need to circle the number against each question. For e.g. if your answer is "Never", the value will be 5 in this section. The final score is calculated towards the end of this exercise.

Good Luck! Remember Answer with 100% honesty for best results.

	PART - B Psychometric Assessment for Creativity Teaching Quotient	5 - Never 4 - Rarely 3 - Sometimes 2 - Most of the Times 1 - Always				
46	I give some special consideration for any one in my class if he/she is my friends or a fellow colleague's son/daughter.	5	4	3	2	1
47	I feel superior than my students who are weak by the virtue of their knowledge and strength.	5	4	3	2	1
48	I consider myself powerful when it comes to judging the students. I prefer the students strictly follow the instructions what I say.	5	4	3	2	1
49	I feel that I am irreplaceable due to my experience, knowledge and the hold I have with my management	5	4	3	2	1
50	Once I frame an impression about a student for say some mistake, I never tend to change it no matter how hard he/she tries to correct him/herself on that mistake.	5	4	3	2	1
51	I have the habit of comparing students in different contexts.	5	4	3	2	1
52	I get distracted easily by non-attentive students. I Ignore them if they approach me for any reason.	5	4	3	2	1
53	I feel bossy, egoistic and authoritative when bunch of students surround my desk in my staff room in the presence of other teachers.	5	4	3	2	1

54	I feel marks is everything. I judge students by the marks they have scored irrespective of their talent.	5	4	3	2	1
55	I raise my voice on a mistake of a student in front of others thinking that it is going to be a lesson for other students.	5	4	3	2	1
56	I enjoy making my students wait for my attention in any public places like staffroom, library, playground, school verandah etc.	5	4	3	2	1
57	I believe being strict is the only way to command respect from students.	5	4	3	2	1
58	I lose my patience when I find students making mistakes repeatedly.	5	4	3	2	1
59	If any of my student happen to be my next-door neighbor, I will strictly keep distance with him/her and will not entertain any contacts.	5	4	3	2	1
60	I prefer to give written imposition as I think that is the only way students will be able to memorize it properly.	5	4	3	2	1

Let us evaluate and see how you have performed in above test. Now sum up all the values and review the results as shown in the following picture.

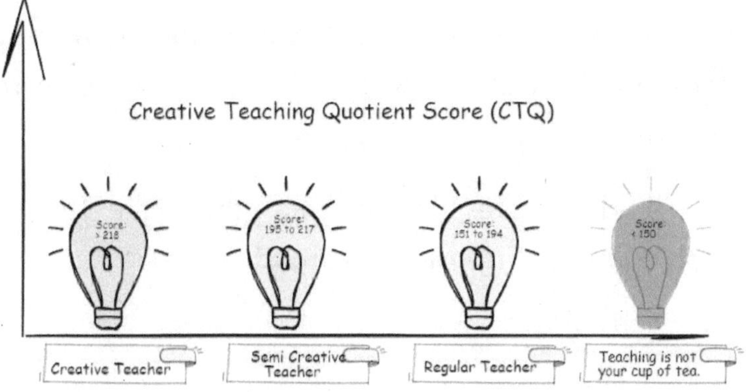

Score: > 218

You are gifted CREATIVE Teacher. A teacher that society needs. Creativity clubbed with resourcefulness make a teacher magical. Your scores are terrific and indicate that you will prove to be an inspiring teacher. Overall, you recognize the importance of developing this skill, in yourself and in children. You are in the unconscious competence quadrant of the Noel Burch's learning competency matrix. competence model (discussed in chapter 4). Teaching is a field that can take a psychological toll on a person. It is quite common for teachers to converse with difficult parents, to deal with difficult children and to have to handle many duties per day as well as long hours. You really seem to have develop the required skills what it takes to deal with these challenges. You have good ability to regulate your feelings and maintain your composure at all times even under moments of emotional struggle. Meditation and Yoga will certainly help you to balance your mind and help you stay creative. There are chances that you become over confident and that becomes detrimental. Staying humble, performing social support will help you to keep you grounded.

Your students are blessed and you make the people involved in your upbringing proud!

Score: 195 to 217

You are on the way to be creative teacher.

You need a good mentor who could help you improve. You are receptive to new information and willing to accept constructive feedback. Being unaware will hold you back. You are in the conscious competence quadrant of the Noel Burch's learning competency matrix. In psychographic terminology, you are in the state of learning, willing to change for good and more of a pragmatist personality.

Identify the weak areas from your low score items and start working over it. You have the potential to encourage, coaching that help bring out the best in others, but may need to make this more of a priority. You are certainly on the right track, just keep it up in your priority list. Reading books, listening to good motivational talks, networking with like minded people will make a huge difference.

Score: 151 to 194

You have a long way to go to be a creative teacher. It is not too late. I am glad that you have started to retrospect which is the first step into change in mindset. You are in the conscious In-competence quadrant of the Noel Burch's learning competency matrix. In other words, you are in the state of awareness. You are able to recognize the deficit and also is aware of the new skill to be learnt that addresses the deficit. You just need the energy to lift yourself and drive. Attending some mindset upliftment and related motivation sessions might help to recharge you. Reading self-help books will help you less distracted. By continuing to develop a strong teacher value, you are more likely to find this career meaningful and fulfilling. There is a Sanskrit term called "guna". Based on the Samkhya philosophy, there are three gunas that influences our physical, mental and emotional state of mind. Based on the result you have good balance of Sattva and Rajas but more dominating guna in "Tamas". Getting into the practice of meditation will immensely ignite the required drive and will balance the gunas.

Score: < 151

Teaching is definitely not your cup of tea. You have chosen this profession for a different purpose that is best known to you. It is in the best interest of yourself, the students and for the country, please introspect your career ambitions and look for other means of income.

Now that you have realized your score and understand where you fit in, it is time you start setting a goal for yourself to improve the score and work towards the goal.

You have come into this field either by passion or don't have any other better ways to earn. Well what ever may be the reason, the first thing you must realize you are a trailblazer for several young minds. You are the guide to the success of students. There has to be compassion filled service. Remember you, through the organization you work for, plays a very key role in the overall development of the children. School education is essential for the overall development of the child. The overall development includes many psychological aspects such as emotions management, positive thinking, handling failures, building the thought process, building confidence, building social skills, maintaining a mental and physical balance, gratitude towards life, empathy towards others, managing the goals, helping them identify their unique strengths etc. What is the point in focusing on a student who top ranks in school but fails miserably in the life. It is the life skills that is more important than academics and that should be the ultimate goal in transformation in the learners though the use of creative coaching techniques.

Creative teachers come with a visionary mindset. They will have a periodic goal to achieve their vision. People often get confused between Vision, goals and wishes. Vision is a milestone.

For e.g. The vision for the teacher may be *"To transform my students with creative thinking abilities through daily student-centered active-learning lessons that enables their academics brilliance with psychological, physical and social well-being"*

Now when you have your visions ready, ask yourself, how am I going to achieve it? Setting goals will help you with this. Goals are set as a specific target that move you towards your vision. This has to be a periodic exercise. Wishes and goals are not the same and neither similar. Goals accompanies a stern action to achieve them. Goals without action remains wishes. If I want to use an equation to summarize the connections between Vision and Action, it will be like the below.

Action with-out Vision = Confusion.

Vision with-out Action = Imagination.

Vision with Action = Transformation.

The purpose of creative teaching is transforming self and the learning members you deal with. The primary reason why most of the learners struggle in their career and at later stage of their life is due to the fact that they were not able to have a goal and they did not have a goal because they haven't identified their strengths. Have you observed, students, during their high schools, doesn't understand what field they want to choose and what works for them. They end up paying for many career counselling sessions with no proper results. The teachers are the first counsellors to the students. If you think you will not do anything above what you are paid which is mainly academics, then you are doing grave injustice to the role you are playing. You might better opt for some other ways to earn your living and not put the student's development at risk.

Let me share a very interesting perspective on the type of teachers and what type of people they mould in this world.

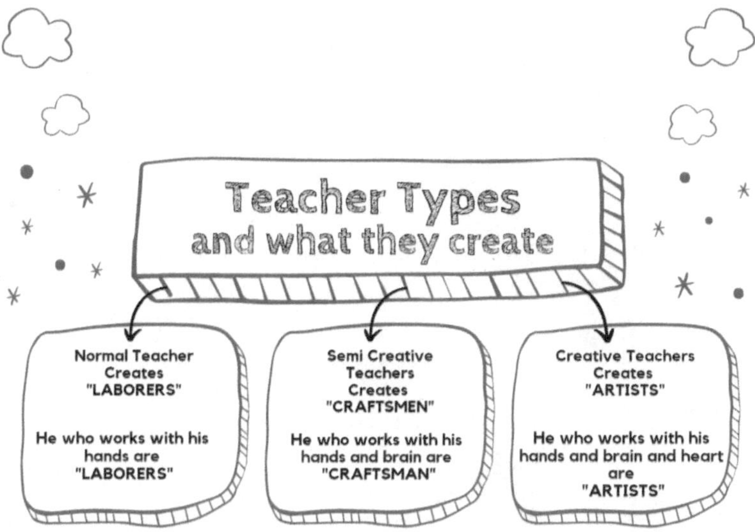

It is the creative teachers who are capable of creating Artists. We need such teachers in the world to add quality, purpose and value to everyone's lives.

4

TAKE THE LEAD. HOW TO TRANSFORM AS A FUTURE READY TEACHER?

"People change their mindset only if they realize it for themselves"

We all want to be the greatest teachers we can be, but the absolute best teacher is not one who knows everything; it's one who is still learning. No matter what your experience level is, there is always bound to be improvement and there is more to learn as a teacher. When you feel like you have nothing more to improve is the moment where your teaching career can be considered as over. The success for teacher to move from a mere teaching to creative teaching starts with the MINDSET. It is the mindset that helps one to reach greater heights.

Eliminate the Mental Blocks – The Cobwebs

The first and foremost step for teachers who are ready and willing to transform is to eliminate the mental blocks.

One of the biggest mental blocks for teachers that prevents them from transforming is the "**Teachers Ego - I K E (I Know Everything)**"

A large part of being a great teacher is character and attitude. I firmly believe that character and attitude cannot be trained by any particular technique, however there are some aspects of one's behavior and personality that can be worked on to improve ourselves as teachers. The biggest of them is ego. Even a great teacher can be derailed by an uncontrolled ego.

Ego can capsize a teacher easily and the danger that I would like to highlight here is that the ego prevents them from learning. You are standing in front of a class of students, a captive audience, you believe you have power over them which is quite a fact. They must listen to what you say. You then control the message and the evaluation of that message in the form grades. I have experienced such teachers during my school days and things have changed a bit now but not drastically.

A good teacher got to be a good learner primarily and let go of the thought of I.K.E. He needs to be a person who is open to new challenges, seeks to improve his art and style of teaching, looks for more interesting ways to engage students, and above all, knows what his students need him to teach. Understanding the needs of the students is the key. It is not what he or she wants to teach or what is easy to teach, but what the students need. Teachers need to focus on creating such a platform for a transformative student learning experience. Do not be a teacher whose ego interferes with their learning. You can learn from your students, your peers even those whom you may think are below you. As a teacher, it's important to remember that when you let your ego rule over you, it is the students that suffer the most. Their learning is severely impacted and to face such setbacks can be much harder to heal.

Egos normally prevent teachers from working together. I see it often. A good team of teachers can accomplish much more than a handful alone, even if they work 20 hours a day. The need of the hour for a future ready teacher is not a competitive mindset but a complementing mindset. A healthy collaboration needs to be inculcated amongst the teachers by sharing lectures, teaching practices, new methods of teaching and any other teaching best practices and get away with the competitive attitude that is prevalent in the educational institution DNA.

Imagine the outcome of a team of teachers who complements his/her colleagues and learn from each other and keeps their focus on your students' learning. I bet they can build and contribute to something that will last forever.

7 Tips to beat Procrastination in Teachers - Why It Matters and How You Can Do It

As a teacher, you are constantly coming up with new ways to reach your students and keep them engaged. However, there's one challenge that almost every educator faces: procrastination. That is the habit of putting off an action to a later time. We all have our moments when we feel like not doing anything. It's frustrating, especially because you know that procrastinating won't get you anywhere in life. But how do we beat this negative habit and make sure we keep moving forward? Let's find out!

Knowing Your Triggers

The first step in overcoming procrastination is knowing your triggers. You need to pay attention to what's going on in your life and how it might be impacting your procrastination. You might not realize it, but certain events, moods, and even locations can cause you to put off your work. Figuring out what these are can help you interrupt the procrastination cycle. It's important to note though that everyone has their own individual triggers that may be different from your colleagues or students. The only way to truly know what's impacting your procrastination is to pay attention to your actions and emotions.

Break the Procrastination Habit

As we mentioned earlier, the first step to overcoming procrastination is understanding it. You need to know why you procrastinate and be able to recognize when you're doing it. Once you're able to recognize the signs of procrastination, you need to break the habit. Here are some tips that might help you break the habit of procrastination. - Identify the task you're avoiding - This can be a daunting task, but you need to identify what it is you're putting off. It could be an essay you have to finish, or it might be planning out your next lesson. Whatever it is, you need to know what it is you're putting off. - Get some help - Sometimes, we need someone else's help to get past our procrastination. If you're having troubles identifying what you need to work on, or if you're feeling uninspired with your work, ask someone for help. - Set a timer - Sometimes, we get stuck in a negative cycle, and we don't know how to get out of it. If you find yourself stuck in a cycle of procrastination, set a timer for 15 or 30 minutes. Focus on the task you need to complete, and don't let yourself get distracted.

Don't Let Fear Hold You Back

Another reason we procrastinate is because we're afraid. It could be something as simple as being afraid to fail, or it could be something as complicated as a phobia. Whatever it is, you need to identify the fear that's holding you back and work to overcome it. You may want to write down your fears and address them one by one. Or, you may want to use some sort of guided visualization to help you confront your fears. You may also want to reach out to a friend or colleague who can help you work through your fears. Collaborating with others can help you overcome your fears, and in turn, help you beat procrastination.

Write Down Your Biggest Aches and Annoyances

Sometimes, we don't know what the root of our procrastination is. Writing down your biggest aches and annoyances can help you identify what's truly plaguing you. Maybe you're frustrated with the curriculum, or maybe you're just having a bad day. Whatever it is, writing down your biggest aches and annoyances can help you get past them. Make sure you're honest with yourself as you write. If you're not being honest with yourself about what's bothering you, you'll never be able to overcome it. Once you've identified your biggest aches and annoyances, you can start to think of ways to address them.

Plan in Advance When You Can

Sometimes, we just don't have the energy to get started on a project or task. If you know that you're prone to procrastinating on a certain assignment or project, make sure you plan in advance when you can work on it. For example, maybe you know you won't have the time to grade a big essay before your weekend. Make sure to plan out when you can grade it so you don't put it off until the very last moment. Planning out your time can help you make sure you don't procrastinate. It can also help you avoid burnout and make sure you're being productive even when you don't feel like it.

Finding New Ways to Celebrate Small Wins

Maybe you've overcome your fear, and you've identified what's holding you back from completing your work, but you still can't seem to stop procrastinating. In this case, you need to find new ways to celebrate small wins. When you celebrate these small wins, you're acknowledging the positives in your life, which can help you stop procrastinating. For example, if you celebrate every time you finish grading one essay, then you'll have plenty of reason to celebrate, and you won't have time to let procrastination get the best of you. Another way to celebrate small wins is to make sure you take small breaks throughout your day. Working for an eight-hour stretch can be extremely tiring, and it can make it easy to procrastinate. If you take breaks throughout your work day, you'll be more likely to stay focused and engaged with your work, which can help you beat procrastination.

The Bottom Line

If you feel like you're always putting things off, you might want to ask yourself why. There are often underlying reasons why people procrastinate, and it's important to face them head on so that you can get back to being productive. Procrastination is a habit that can be hard to break. It can be frustrating, especially when you know you're capable of so much more. However, with some self-reflection, you can overcome the habit of procrastination. It all starts with knowing your triggers, breaking the habit, and making sure you don't let fear hold you back.

The Comfort Zone and Teaching Habits – An Activity

Our habits are like an automated driver that helps us do everything without too much thinking.

Habits help make it easy to get things done quickly with conscious application of our mind. This means we don't have to think too hard about how to execute our routine tasks, we simply do them habitually because it works. New ways of doing things, like social distancing, challenge us but begin to be habitual instincts in time. Getting more conscious of the way we do things however will help us be as adaptable and flexible as we can be and also prevent us slipping into any unhelpful habits in challenging times.

Trying something new can seem scary and not worth the effort and that is because you are habituated to stay comfortable. Comfort zone is the killer of your growth and below are some practical ways that helps you to step out of it.

Close your eyes and consciously take 25 cycles of deep breaths. One Inhale/Exhale is considered one full cycle.

Figure out at what cycle, you are getting distracted. Try to increase the distraction stages by consistent practice. You may experience the distraction as early as the 2nd cycle itself. Not to worry, start over and continue the practice till you feel a complete control over your distraction.

When you feel in complete control over these breathing cycles, you can shift the gear now. After say around 10 cycles, begin your introspection journey.

Think what is stopping you from the change, what habits are limiting you.

Prepare your mind to get comfortable with discomfort. Imagine moments of discomfort and how you have overcome it in the past.

As you continue to breath, imagine your system is undergoing version upgrades just like computer does.

Imagine the people you know who have taken risks and how it has benefitted them.

Visualize yourself in that role and feel how you as a person would have done things differently.

Tell multiple times to yourself to never take the result to your heart and head, be it success or failures.

Fill your mind with optimism like a juice being poured in to your glass.

By now you would have taken many breathing cycles. Become aware of your surroundings and bring your attention back to the present and slowly open your eyes. Feel the new version of yourself.

Continue this practice atleast once a day. Note that when you reach in your 60s, 70s and beyond, you should not feel regret for not trying something amazing in your life. Those are the days one should feel good and enjoy thinking about the milestones and accomplishments. So, gear up, get started and rock!

Victim Mindset

More worrying are the unconscious habits of thinking that hold some teachers, and therefore their pupils, back. Amongst these are the 'victim' mentality, believing the world is against them, fixed mindset teacher who finds training of any kind is a massive waste of time. Think of your staffroom and those whose demeanor and conversation habitually, unconsciously drain you of any optimism for the future. Think also of those others who lift our mood with their optimism and sense of humor. Which one are you? How can you find out? Becoming aware of our own habits of thinking is the first step towards self-awareness.

"This is not doable, I am just a small part of the system",

"I am willing to change, but the protocols would not let me do it"

"I need to just obey the orders else I will lose my job"

"My hands are tied and I have my limitation to bring in what I want"

Does the above set of statements sound familiar to you or heard it from your inner voice? This is quite natural. Yes, we have limitations, challenges, road blocks but end of the day it is up to us to find out ways through strategic sense to stretch and bring in the change we want to see. Teachers of today should get out of the victim mindset.

I have shared several best teaching practices through-out this book that can be thought through and apply them. They are well within the limitations of the system. However, I am just opening your minds to enable the creative sense to look at things. The Bhagwat Gita says "Life is not fair and easy on anybody but what is Right (Dharma) is known to your Mind (conscience). No matter how much unfairness and limitations we undergo, how many times we were disgraced, how many times we fall, what is important is how you reacted at that time. The unfairness that you deal with your education management or system that you are part of, does not give you license to be rigid or have a fixed mindset. Always remember life may be tough at few points, but DESTINY is not created by the SHOES we wear but by the STEPS we take.

Sprout Yourself – GROW from within!

There will be times when you as a teacher feel stuck in the role you play or in the organization you work. You feel some one has buried you in. Over a period of time, teachers get used to the culture and slowly get into that comfort zone. Here is where you switch your creative cells on and find ways to improve your skill, add more value to your knowledge, create your own brand of teaching. I have analogically portrayed that in the above picture. Even when you feel you are buried, you can still continue to grow from within and it is only a matter of time, you will march on to the path of becoming a self-sustained teacherpreneur!

Let us find out from the below image on the characteristics of a fixed teaching mindset vs that of a growth teaching mindset.

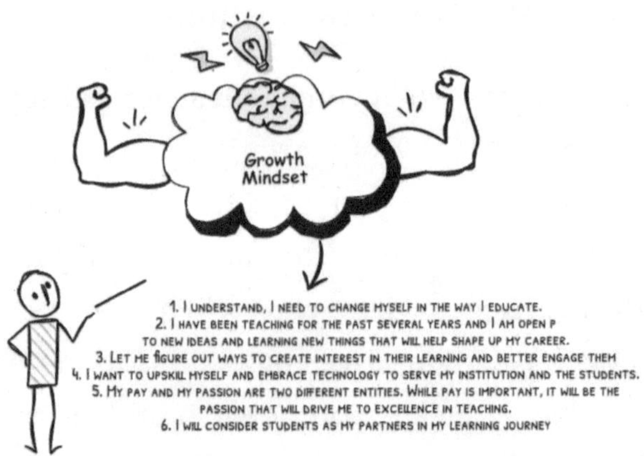

Stop using the term "Soft Skill". There is no such thing!

Students will need cognitive skills like critical and creative thinking, collaboration and communication with people and researchers all over the world to be future ready. It is the growth mindset that will help teachers to transform to be future ready teacher. First thing they need to do is to stop using the term Soft skills. The term soft skills are so deep rooted in our society that the true sense of it has been buried. Just by googling you will see that it means skills that relate your personality be in Inter personal, communication, time management empathy etc. Now please give a deep thought to it. Aren't these really the must have skills more than anything else. How can something as essential as communication and inter personal skills be called as soft.

Reflective Teaching Habits!

One of the hottest topics in education circles these days is reflective teaching. This method borrows ideas from anthrozoology that have been applied to animal training, and it uses feedback loops to shape student behavior. Reflective teaching has many attributes that teach students better, including addressing learners' needs for motivation and content relevance. Teachers are using it to promote active learning for students which exposes them to new material. It allows students to construct their own understanding and skills in the study of their subject. Teachers who employ reflective teaching have seen some staggering benefits over their peers, such as less incidence of boredom among students, more motivation to learn, and greater retention rates.

This type of teaching envisions teachers as "facilitators during the learning process, not just instructors." A world without a teacher lecturing up front. This could be considered an innovative solution for those struggling in school because it makes them feel seen and valued. By asking students questions about their lessons and forcing them to offer solutions, it provides students the opportunity to reflect on what they have learned throughout the course of the lesson. As a result, the student will have more time to think critically about what they are learning and be more engaged in class.

The digitized world of today demands the educators to be more reflective than ever before. There are three different ways that instructors can incorporate reflection into their teaching: 1) Reflection with the curriculum, 2) Reflection with their students, 3) Reflection on their own teaching style

Students are motivated to learn when they can see themselves progressing shape and skill. Others become inspired by seeing how they might be able to apply their knowledge in the real world. Reflective teaching allows teachers to share their reasoning, successes and struggles with students so that they are not just shown what's right but also the full spectrum of possibilities in teaching thus help students learn more and promote self-awareness.

Educational institutes, this message is exclusively for you!

Every educational institution should invest in regular skill development workshops for teachers. They need to be motivated to become coaches, who can influence the learners, who can value diversity, who can embrace the change and establishes a trailblazer culture. Reward the teachers who deliver strong performances.

Stop the fake process demands. In my last seven digital transformation workshops that I had facilitated for teaching community during the times of pandemic, I realized that most of them joined the session just to attain a mere certificate of completion as that has become a measuring criterion by the educational organizations that have hired them. They go in the mute mode and do other non-productive activities or remain just mute spectators. What is the message they are giving and what is the point in even attaining such certifications that has no value than a quantified representation of a fake performance? The management should set a platform and give the freedom and platform to teachers to improvise their current skills. There are many tangible ways to track the performance of the teachers.

Make Learning interesting. Get away with practices that make it boring!

These days, it appears that it isn't much about learning. It seems to be all about tests, grades, and your school's average grade or percentage. I believe many students aren't really gaining any knowledge. Grades are determining how smart we are or what schools or colleges we qualify to enter. Should the grades determine this? But we don't have a choice. The education eco system in many developing countries continues this grading system. I believe it is the only measuring system to gauge the knowledge today. Everybody is smart in their own way. Some teachers only care about themselves, their reputations, and how they look at their school. Also, some teachers move on from lesson to lesson without taking the time to pause and see if their students actually understand what they are taught. It ends up in the way that students tend to pass more than actually learn. Our investment to get educated determines how far we'll get in life.

This education system doesn't provide financial knowledge to us so our mindset just focuses on 9 to 5 jobs. We don't want to learn. Now we are happy with this system because we don't want what actually we want to do. We say that now there are no opportunities. Actually, there are millions of opportunities available but we don't have any knowledge about them. Our education system doesn't provide us such knowledge. The education system is failing and really needs improvement. Change your mindset now if we will not do something for us today then we are also one of them who always complain about opportunities in the years to come.

Stop being a mood driven teacher!

Mood of the teacher influences a lot within the students. Have you experienced a conversation like this? *"Hey, Devika ma'am seems quite upset, don't ask questions today"* or *"Shrikant sir is in angry mood, let us not discuss the math homework doubts now"*. I have experienced it many times during my school and college days. This only goes on to tell that teachers, when driven by mood, upsets the whole learning condition for the student at that moment. The child learns this behavior stint without even being aware of it and applies them when he turns adult. A teacher is a human and might undergo mix of emotions from the dawn to dusk. It is important for them to keep their emotions away to an extent that it doesn't impact the children by any ways. Turn the maturity level up to overcome this emotional baggage.

Stop trying to be favorite!

Every teacher wants to be the favorite amongst the students, they enjoy the attention, the power over them and the overall control. However, students generally tend to be fickle minded. If you have students who display a bad attitude, whether it's towards you or towards learning in general, don't take it personally. When you take things personally, you basically risk of letting your dark side take over. The worst thing you can do is make enemies inside the classroom. When you allow your students' behavior to affect your own mood, it can be very difficult to rescue the student–teacher relationship afterwards.

Don't put the blame on the students!

It's important to note that the time you spend with your students is very limited during the day, and they have so much going on in their lives that you are not even aware of. This is the reason why I have dedicated a separate section on KYS (Know your student) in chapter 7. On a particular day, when you encounter a student behaving out of character, there's quite a possibility that it has nothing at all to do with you at all. Let us not antagonize the student nor try too hard to cheer them up either. Keep your focus on delivering a great lesson in the hopes that it will engage any problematic students, but as long as there's no disruption to the lesson, let them have their space. This is particularly important for your adolescent / young adult students. Teacher need to show them some respect by letting them have their personal space which they will appreciate it for sure. Apply the creative teaching techniques mentioned in the last chapter of this book and engage them to cheer up and participate, and they are more likely rise up to the occasion. On the other hand, you may also encounter students who are consistently negative, consider approaching them on neutral ground and finding out if there's anything in particular that they're having trouble with. It's essential that you avoid public confrontation with them. The fact is that we don't know what their lives hold.

Speak with the student softly while the class is occupied, or else find a time outside of the classroom to convene with him in a non-threatening way. Do this without blame or accusation but also without trying too hard to relate. Ask if there's anything he needs help with or anything he would like to see more of in your lessons. Ultimately, just make it clear that you are there to support his learning. With this approach we have a much better chance of creating a connection.

Teach your students not only the ways to succeed but also the ways to grow through failures!

It is the responsibility of the teacher to teach their children not only the ways to succeed but ways to grow through failures. Let us first accept that failures are inevitable. There is always lots of experiences from failure behind the success of any person. The other side always looks green, everywhere we look, other's achievement loom large. The society we live in pushes us to paint a rosy picture of accomplishments to gain respect and value. Take a look at the social media posts, it is all rosy picture of achievements that you can find. I am not demeaning painting the rosy picture, but there are several stories of failures and struggles behind those stories which is never portrayed. The path to success is shaped by failures. It must be noted that failing at something allows one to do a deep retrospection, reflect, and develop new perspectives. It simply pushes us to start operating from inside our strength zone but outside of our comfort zone.

Some of the teachers have the bad habit to generate fear on failures. In their efforts to prepare students for success, they end up taking away a valuable opportunity of letting the students, learn from their mistakes, learn to take calculated risks, finding ways to step out of their comfort zone and most importantly learn to manage challenging feelings and negative emotions. Many successful personalities have spoken about the lessons taught by failure.

They had ideas that they put into motion when they were rejected. A classic example is the story of Brian Acton, the co -founder of WhatsApp, the social media messaging services giant. Brian had applied for a job at Facebook in 2009 and was rejected. In 2014 exactly five years after that rejection, his widely used platform was bought by Facebook for a whopping 19 billion dollars making him vividly rich. The simple mantra that he applied was tuning himself with a growth mindset, which allowed him to believe that he has not achieved his purpose with yet. This only tells us that no matter how many times one may fail, but as long as they redirect their energy creatively and constructively, no situation can just stop them from achieving their goals of life.

Another interesting story is that of J.K. Rowling the world-famous author of the Harry Potter series. In her speech at Harvard, she talks about the benefits of failure. She says some of failure in life is inevitable and that it is impossible to live without failing at something, unless you live so cautiously that you might as well not have lived at all – in which case, you fail by default.

According to her, it is the failure that gave her that inner security which she could have never attained by passing any sort of examinations. It taught her more things about herself. She further quotes that *"The knowledge that you have emerged wiser and stronger from setbacks means that you are, ever after, secure in your ability to survive. You will never truly know yourself, or the strength of your relationships, until both have been tested by adversity. Such knowledge is a true gift, for all that it is painfully won, and it has been worth more than any qualification I ever earned"*.

She is an inspiration to many in the way she used failures as a stepping stone to her super successful journey. If you turn around and see the people, there will be many who had the courage to sail through the turbulence caused in their lives and we as teachers, must teach such examples to uplift the students consistently.

Teach them Happiness Mantras!

The Purpose of life is to be Happy. Happiness is nothing but "the state of being happy". It is very difficult to say what actually makes someone happy. Happiness is not a spiritual term, it is something to be understood and inculcated into the minds of students right from the school and college days. Many problems that one is facing today is due to the lack of awareness about the term happiness. Let us see the quotes of few spiritual leaders around happiness.

"True happiness lies in dedicating one's life to the cause of the less fortunate and not in material wealth" – Dalai Lama

"The path to true happiness lies in "other-centered behavior" and that "material things do not bring happiness" - Oswald Cardinal Gracias

"Happiness manifests when you feel free from within" – Sri Sri Ravishankar.

"Happiness" is the ultimate freedom" from suffering" – Gautam Buddha.

"The great secret of true success, of true happiness, is this: the man or woman who asks for no return, the perfectly unselfish person, is the most successful." – Swami Vivekananda

"Happiness in the Qur'an refers to a permanent state in paradise and not a state of mere physical joy in this world."

"True joy is a by-product, not a goal" – Bible Teacher – Dr. David Jeremiah.

"Joy is a natural phenomenon, misery is your creation – Sadhguru.

Below are excerpts from the teachings of His holiness Dalai Lama on finding the true happiness.

We all wish to be more like children, who are naturally good at being in the present moment. They have natural tendencies to accepting of others. It is the joy of little things that keep the children happy. As we grow into the adulthood, we ignore to nurture our natural potential and get caught up in secondary differences of the "us" vs "them". Our model of teaching should change this. We need to learn and teach to distinguish the destructive nature of emotions like anger, fear and attachment, which disturb the peace of mind. Teach them the positive qualities of compassion even if that is to smile another human being.

The world today is mostly focused on external development. However, ancient Indian traditions emphasize looking within to find the real source of joy. Being joyful is a skill to be first learnt by the teacher and to be taught to the students.

The Kindergarten teachers would be learning more about the joyous nature from her little kids than what the kids learn from the teachers. It might sound funny but is the fact. Cultivate an attitude of happiness within the students. Life has ups and downs and, in every circumstance, it is the duty of the teacher to develop the determination to not let anything in the world disrupt the happiness. They need to set themselves as role models. That is the purpose of wisdom.

If one student in a class is unhappy, it affects every other student directly or indirectly. We are all interdependent on, and interconnected with, one another as humans. Though happiness is an individual attitude, it is also linked to our environment and creating such a joyous environment reflects the functioning of a true creative teacher.

As teachers, you don't have to literally preach anything about happiness from the texts to make it look boring rather engage them in the practices that will be more fun. This will develop the sense of happiness even without their knowledge. This is where act of creativity comes for teacher. The practices that one may be able to apply in the classroom for developing the happiness quotient is discussed in the chapter 7.

Open to continuous Learning!

Let us understand the relationship between learning and teaching. The best way to learn something is to teach and the best way to teach something is to learn. They are tightly coupled entities. People assume that that one needed to be taught on "how to learn something". That is not entirely correct. Learning may happen without teaching but the reverse cannot be true. Most of our learning happens unconsciously. There is a process called unconscious installation which depicts learning of something without being taught formally.

For e.g.

We learn by watching others do things either by formally sitting or working alongside someone else, or even just by noting what someone else does.

We learn from the advices of others.

We learn by listening to audios, reading books and social media posts & blogs, watching videos.

Most of all, we experiment and learn by doing. In our day to day experiences we, often unconsciously, review, draw conclusions, conceptualize and form our belief system.

The consequences of our learning or our failure to learn have a direct impact on our lives.

Learning a new skill using the conscious competence ladder!

Let me introduce you to an interesting framework called as Conscious Competence Learning Model. This matrix model explains four stages of learning any new skill. Noel Burch an employee of the Gordon Training International introduced this model in the early 1970s.

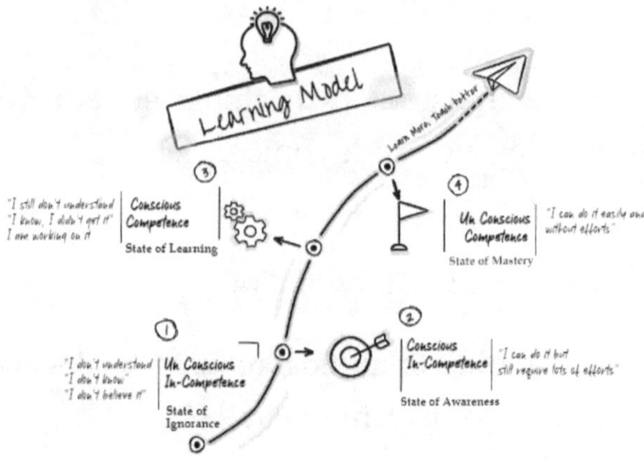

When you really understand Burch's learning stages, it makes it much easier to add to your skill set. The Psychometric score that we discussed in the chapter three will help you understand the stage where you are currently placed. The stages make an absolutely reliable template for improving yourself in any skill area. The model highlights two factors that affect our thinking as we learn a new skill: consciousness (awareness) and skill level (competence).

The learning journey begins at stage 1 - 'unconscious incompetence'. They then pass through stage 2 - 'conscious incompetence', then through stage 3 - 'conscious competence' finally the stage 4 - 'unconscious competence' where learning comes naturally to you without any additional efforts. The learning becomes a habit at this stage. Let us understand the stages little bit more.

Unconscious incompetence – (Ignorance)

In this stage, say if the teacher is not good at something but is ignorant about it. He/She does not necessarily recognize that there is a deficit. In this case, there is never going to be learning! This is why when we need to mentor teachers to make them realize their shortcoming. They must first recognize their own incompetence, and the realize the value of the new skill. The moment they realize that, he/she is ready for the next stage.

Conscious incompetence (Awareness)

Though the teacher does not understand or know how to do something, he or she does recognize the deficit and the value of a new skill in addressing the deficit. The making of mistakes can be integral to the learning process at this stage. Psychologically, to many teachers, this stage is the most uncomfortable, since they have to realize that they are not carrying out a certain activity properly. Acknowledging the short comings lead to feelings of embarrassment, so they tend to ignore and be back to the stage 1 as it is considered as secure zone.

Conscious competence (Learning)

This is the stage where learning actually happens. The teacher understands or knows how to do something. They actively look forward ways to improve the skill. However, demonstrating the skill or knowledge requires focus and experimenting mindset that is marked by trying things, failing, trying again, and getting better. With consistent efforts, the competence will only grow. Sooner or later you will find this new skill becoming part of your day to day routine. The key for this stage is to persevere and not give up.

Unconscious competence (Mastery)

The individual has had so much practice with a skill that it has become "second nature" or automatic and can be performed easily without even applying any extra efforts. As a result, the skill can be performed while executing another task. The individual may be able to teach it to others, depending upon how and when it was learned. The individual has then developed the state of unconscious competence. As much as it is the desirable state of mind that every teacher aspires, it also throws some psychological dangers in this segment because at some point we just assume we are doing something well and forget to notice when we are not. They might become vulnerable to complacency and cease to be learners. One must be mindful of these unconscious traits and explore ways to tackle them creatively. Attending regular leadership workshops, motivational seminars and training on related topics would help to maintain the rhythm.

Let us take for example – The driving of a car. Some people will not feel the need to drive the car as they don't think it is necessary for them (this is unconscious incompetence). As the situation demands, people will then realize the need and enroll themselves into a driving school knowing that they have it all to learn (conscious incompetence). As they progress, they learn the techniques but are conscious of what they are doing, especially the driving test! (That will be the conscious competence.) Having passed the test and been driving for a few years, most of us are driving on autopilot when we get into our cars (this is the unconscious competence stage). This is where complacency kicks in if we don't act on time, people get overconfident, attend phones while driving, or make purposeful mistakes that become detrimental.

Do you remember the conscious incompetence you felt teaching your first lesson? That feeling of being unsure, panicky and that you recollect every instruction and mistakes you did. Then after much practice though you eventually moved to conscious competence, still learning, and eventually through to unconscious competence where things became so much easier and learned the habits.

Now the question that arises is, did you learn good or bad habits? Bad teaching habits can develop, often unconsciously – too much teacher talk, ignoring the invisible child, favoritism, ignoring bad behavior, arriving late to lessons etc. At first, when these bad habits are mentioned in performance management meetings, you might have tried to change but over consistent similar feedbacks, the ignorance kicks in and you would stop caring about them. These bad habits are easy to solve though, through mindfulness, awareness and cultivating open to change mindset.

Listed below are some of the day to day examples in learning. As a small activity, place yourself in one of the stages where you feel you are best placed at this point of time.

- Preparing your favorite food.
- Tying your shoes
- Preparing a Power point presentation
- Meditation
- Taking money from ATM
- Singing
- Depositing a cheque at your bank,
- Public speaking

Once you get a solid understanding of this model, you might want to take it with your students. Place them in the respective stages of their learning. Do not measure their knowledge only through marks, rather their competence and help them progress through the stages till learning becomes a habit and comes naturally to them. Please note that the students only respond to training when they are aware of their own need for it, and the personal benefit they will derive from achieving it. When you make them realize it in a manner that they can corelate, you become successful as a teacher coach. A good teacher is like a coach. He knows how to bring out the best in his students. He knows when to push them and when to let them rest. He knows what they are capable of and he challenges them to do their best.

There is a feeling of awakening when students move from one stage to another. Associate it with a reward or points system which is only meant for them and not to be publicly discussed. Give them a sense of accomplishment as they move towards the next stage. Remember, the whole purpose of my book is not to be used as prescription rather build on the topics discussed and create workable models out of it. This model is super helpful in addressing the teaching obstacles. You will know what is making a student stuck at a particular stage of learning.

The theory of conscious competence helps both teachers and learners to get a grip on why an obstacle exists, and what best needs to be done to deal with the challenge. This encourages assessment at an individual level and sets up a personalized development path, which is normally overlooked when so much learning and development being delivered at a group level.

Be Receptive to new ideas!

As you move through your career, you'll work alongside many teachers from all sorts of different backgrounds.

The best way to develop as a teacher is to take every opportunity to learn from fellow colleagues around you not only from your institution but also networking with peers outside. There will always be some new ideas or best practices in teaching that may learn from others even if they have lesser experience than you. Learn to seek feedback be it from a fellow teacher or someone senior or even from a student. Some new ideas will strike you and you can look for any elements that you can salvage and incorporate it into your teaching practice that will help you to transform holistically as a future ready teacher. You end up creating your own "Teaching Brand".

So, in summary, your future readiness journey can be applied in six practical steps.

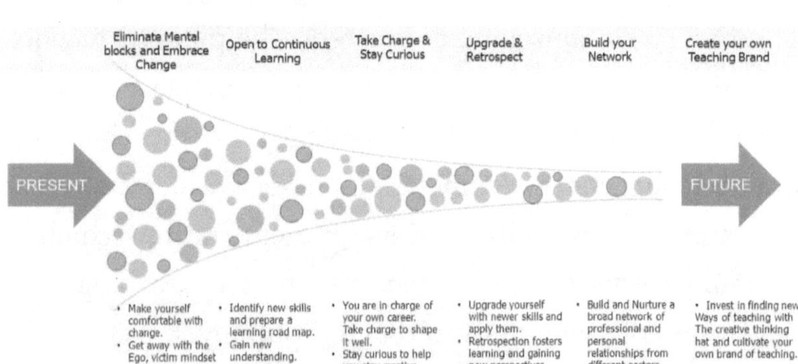

5

THE PANDEMIC FACTOR, GADGETS AND THE ONLINE CLASSES. THE IMPACT

"Teaching kids to count is fine, but teaching them what counts is best"

The Covid-19 pandemic has resulted in a complete shutdown of schools across the world. It has sent the planet into a tail-spin. Going by the statistics more than 1.2 billion children in 186 countries have been adversely affected by school closures that has resulted in a paradigm shift in school education to e-learning. Parents and teachers who have long seen them as supplementary learning tools have started to adopt them as mainstream education platforms.

There is a school of thought that online learning takes less time and it has been shown to increase retention of information. The effectiveness of online medium actually depends on the way student adopts to this new practice and the way the online classes are conducted.

At the beginning of the pandemic, I witnessed that many of the teachers found it struggling to handle classes, the primary reason for that was they were being judged and that they started to get more conscious of their teaching abilities. They felt when the students are engaged through the online sessions, the parents also witnessed it. Teachers felt their preparation time for online sessions was 3x more than the offline preparation. Their capabilities were tested big time. They had to build new skills to adjust to this new mode of teaching.

In the current scenario, Teachers and the educational institutions need to act beyond academics to teach students life skills such as resilience that will see them through testing times like the pandemic. Students need to be taught to make plans but be flexible about it and prep them to handle when things go wrong. We need to teach them to think as leaders by making them resolve small issues thorough objective thinking and make decisions with utmost sensitivity and simplicity. They need to be coached with better crisis management, racial tolerance and how to be happy and at peace with themselves.

Sometimes teaching children about crafts and trades like electric wiring, carpentry, gardening, wall painting, knitting etc. does stimulates their creativity and provide them with choices later, whether that is to supplement their income or as a career option. I was very much interested in electric wiring and used to learn by seeing my uncle setting up wiring in the house. Let me share an interesting story from my childhood. This is the story about something I learned by just watching my uncle do it. My Uncle was an expert in electric wiring, motor wiring and pretty much deals with every type of electric system set up.

He is not a certified or an authorized electrician. I discovered my interest in working with electricity during those times. I visit my native during every school vacation. It is a located in a remote village in central part of Kerala. This place was prone to electric failures particularly during thunder storms. Getting an authorized electrician at that time was very difficult. It used to take at least a week for the electricity to be restored in such circumstances.

Once during a stormy night, we experienced an unexpected power outage. As expected, my uncle got into the act. He used a blue thick wire to connect one end to the electric pole and the other to the live line in the motor shed. As it used to be quite dark, I assisted him with torch lights. Once it got connected, the lights were on. That is how practically I learned the concept behind parallel circuit. As I grew up a similar incident occurred while my uncle was not around. I, in all confidence, rose to the occasion and applied the learning to the surprise of my home mates. When I think back such situations, I realize it was the kind of learning by watching someone do it. Of-course my interest in wiring made the job easy.

Even today, I enjoy setting up many things on electricity at my home. Although it is not a career option, I still do it. These are all the facts teachers should encourage the students to do while they focus on the job in hand. It saved me lots of money, considering the labor work that would have been needed. It is such art that makes one find ways to happiness. Nothing that you learn will ever go waste. It could be used at some stage of one's life for sure. I would even recommend to teach some productive labor work such as book binding, soap or candle making or recycled products and cooking as well.

Typical anxiety issues faced by Teachers during the online classes.

With this pandemic kicking in, it gave birth to new terms in our everyday conversations like lockdown, pandemic, Covid-19, social distancing, double masking etc. which were something most of us never heard before. Our way of thinking, working, living, eating, studying, conversing, thinking has been changed radically. Every single person on the planet has been affected by these changes. The education industry was hugely taken by a shock, much like the rest of the world. The only difference was that in this sector the children and their futures were at play. Our student population in the country is the largest in the world.

Students from ages 5 to 21 had their lives toppled when they suddenly had to figure out ways to learn something without face to face interaction and that they had to rely in the on the screens that no one was yet comfortable with. During the initial days of pandemic, every teacher adopted a trial and error approach and structured their teaching formats and styles of handling classes in line with what worked best for them and their students.

At the time of writing this book, I have seen that the teachers have finally found their footing in handling online sessions more effectively. While most teachers are eager to go back to the way things were, a few of them see merit in the way things are being done right now. For e.g. When you are online on a screen facing 25+ other kids, there is no faking attention anymore unlike the offline mode. Isn't that something every teacher wishes for? It is easy to identify students who lacks attention. Teachers are finding ways to hold their students' attention, while having to cope with not only their own technological issues but also of their students. In others ways this whole set back have forced the teaching fraternity to look at new and improved ways of teaching. It has been a constructive learning experience for both teachers and students.

There are ups and downs to online education. The advantage is that students were able to learn in their own zone of comfort and at their own pace. Students who were less interactive have gained the confidence to interact during online classes through the chat messages with their videos off. Some students are seen to socialize with their buddies in schools. It motivates them to go to schools physically and play with their peers rather than stay closed at homes. For them, online education may not be that effective but for students who are academically inclined wish to defy all the odds and accepts online medium as an effective platform. While teachers have been busy trying to complete their academic portions and grading them, what left unnoticed are the frustration levels that have been building up among the students as a result of the extended periods of lack of interaction with their buddies.

The psychologists and experts believe that the minor inconveniences that we seem to feel in today's scenario, could potentially translate to bigger issues in the future. It could be anywhere from difficulty in social interaction to lack of easy access to higher education to even employability, the future could see challenges in various sizes and shapes. The impact that these months have had on their psyche is something that will only be clearer in the years to come. This means that teachers will now have to be all the more focussed on the student's overall well being.

The chapter 7 talks in detail about what is expected out of them in order to generate a mentally, physically, morally, emotionally healthly and creative community of students. I strongly believe that it is the creative community that builds social fabric of the society. If you are just teaching the subject that is good enough but if you tell something which makes them think., which makes them ponder, which sensitizes them, then that becomes great. It enables teachers to achieve their personal fulfillment.

Education experts and academicians are continually pondering over the fact whether online learning will continue to persist and what will be its cascading impact on the worldwide education sector.

Artificial intelligence has been playing a pivotal role in almost every field, including the education sector. The AI based learning platforms have been on the rise since the evolution of the smart phone era and has exponentially shot up since the beginning of pandemic. These adoptions have helped both students and teachers in personalized learning experience. Many of students finds it quite interesting, rewarding and engaging. There is no one size fits all concept in learning any more due the personalization factors the AI based models are providing. One can adjust the pace of learning based on their individual choice and preferences which helps them to attain higher scores. Tech companies are roping in tech savvy grads to help students learning lessons, finish homework's outside school.

One must note that these tech-based learning companies are making the learning more personalized using the artificial intelligence techniques that includes observing the learning behavior of the student. They generate graphs to let the parent know about the child's progress. What the technology cannot replace is the emotional and personal touch with a real time teacher. So, it becomes all the more important for the teacher to survive in the tech dominated learning management systems and that is possible only if they take the creative route and stay ahead of the technology.

Two architect grads from Chennai created a unique online mentoring platform namely mentor match to help students from class 3 to 10 to match with a perfect mentor of their choice. They don't have to study alone. It offers a study buddy. A great initiative and the need of the hour. The uniqueness about this platform is students tend to learn from their peers who have found innovative ways to learn the same concepts. It is quite different from our conventional tuition classes where is it completely subject and study focused. For e.g. if it is a Class VIII music-loving space scientist aspirant, they match him to another student who has the same taste. That helps to keep the child motivated. Most students know what to learn, but lose their way when it comes to how to study.

Mentors and study buddies can help students find a smart, fast and efficient way to go about it. There are several such start up initiatives which looks into solving a social issue. Now my perspective here is if two grads can think of something like why can't the teachers think of something like this for their organization, for their classes? I am sure every institution throws different challenges to its teachers. If they have really a good break through idea, they can rather prepare a case, publicize this though a social media and get the attention from the right stake holders who can help implement the solution. For that thinking to happen, they need to come out of the typical subject and portion completion mindset and get into the creative teaching journey.

Technology's Increasing Role in Education and Skill Development

If you go back to the days prior to the Covid-19, the adoption of technology in education was very minimal. For most of the educational institutions, technology was meant as setting up a computer lab with an outdated curriculum being followed.

It is quite evident by now that the launch of newer technologies and electronic gadgets has played an important role in transforming the education sector in many ways. The interesting catch is that when education is coupled with technology, both students and teachers find it more interesting as the imparting the knowledge and experience becomes all the more engaging. The Internet has played a key role in making technology more accessible to common people. Technology is the most imperative element of our lives. Any business or economy cannot grow without support from the technology. Its importance is now quite visible in almost every sector including education.

Educational institutions are now using technology and electronic gadgets for teaching, which makes their work much easier. Technology has become an instructional delivery system, helps us with means of aiding instructions, and also acts as a tool to enhance the entire learning process. The pandemic boosted it further.

As a creative teaching evangelist and teacher coach, I am constantly in admiration of their commitment and their determination to make a difference to the younger generation of students. End of the day what really matters is what teachers say and do in classrooms to help learners grow into creative, adaptable, self-reliant, resilient and compassionate people.

6

DEALING THE GENERATION Z STUDENTS. SHIFT THE GEARS!

"Teacher's job is not to prepare students for something. Their job is to help them prepare for anything." - A.J. Juliani

We can't deny the fact the social media system of today is making children more and more self-centered. Using social media needs maturity and maturity only comes with age. The students need to be inculcated with proper skills to use the technology and social media in the truest sense. While in most countries we have an age restriction to attain a driver's license while we don't have any such criteria to gain access to social media. The difference is that the former is physical while the latter is more mental but both results in accidents if not properly managed.

As a result, it becomes all the more important for the teachers to see the bigger picture of the changing times and channelize their attention to focus on honing the new-age skills that includes building a culture of mindfulness and higher self-esteem.

In my regular conversations with fellow parents and teachers, I have heard concerns about their kids being addicted to phones, social media, video streaming, gaming etc. and succumbing to dangers. The big mistake parents do here is they shut their complete access to the internet. You must understand that everybody in his/her world will be on the phones and restricting their access is going to take a tough toll on them and should be avoided. The most ideal way is to build their self-esteem. Studies have shown that students succumb to internet dangers when he/she feels insecure. Make sure he/she is confident about who and what they are, make sure they are not overly reliant on how he/she looks. You are not able to baby sit and watch them continuously. If you make him/her feel amazing the way he/she is they will not succumb to other people. This is where Parents and Teachers both play a major role in the life of a child particularly the Gen-Z.

This book helps you adopt newer, faster, more effective forms of teaching, which also means training your brain to think and act in new ways.

Not many are aware that that there is a categorization of students by generations namely Generation X, Y and Z. A table that defines these generations and the facts associated with them are list in the below figure

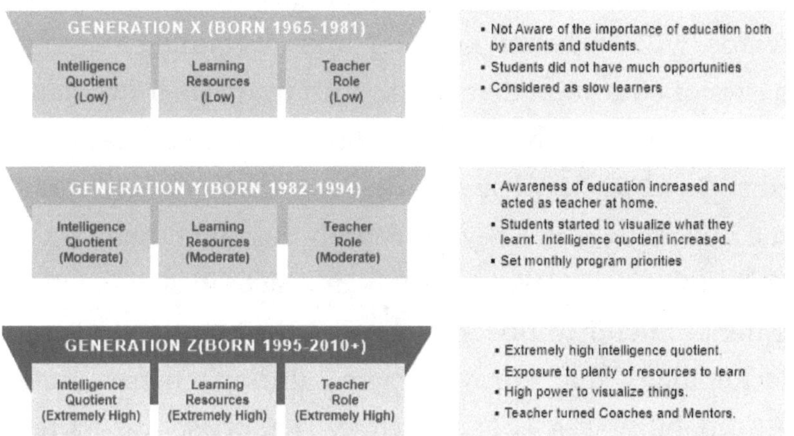

Generation X

The role of a teacher in the current generation is to not just meant to teach the curriculum or subject they are allotted to its students rather to mentor them with various new age resources which they were not exposed to and help them to seamlessly absorb in their system. The role of a teacher is shifting the gears from the practices that were adopted from Generation X, Generation Y and to Generation Z.

Gen X. This is the industrial revolution stage.

Earlier the role of a teacher for the Generation X type students were impart the knowledge of the basics, fundamentally about importance of being educated as they weren't aware about it. The teacher influenced the caretakers of the student with the information that their wards will be better position upon obtaining the right basics of education that will in turn uplift their life status. Gen X did not have much opportunities. They were considered as slow learners due to the lack of exposure to the outside world. They grew with the same thought that their role is to take up the same activities what their parents intend to do. As one can imagine, they were no technology that drove them during those times. Affordability was a big challenge. That phase was more of people finding ways to survive. They took a job purely for survival so that their basic necessities such as food, clothes and shelter are met. As a result, they got employed in a place and wouldn't leave their workplace even if the boss was abusive. That was the era of "bosses always right", because opportunities were less. They are pretty much the grandparents of today's workforce.

Generation Y

Gen Y: This is the information age.

Then came the Information Revolution, where the corporate culture was born. Here the workforce came to work but the purpose was not for survival. Their parents from Gen X took care of survival. This workforce went to work for improving their standard of living, getting into a good enough salary to build the house, buy cars, better education for children, usage of electronics etc. If you comparatively see, the loyalty was reduced as there are more options to choose.

A Teacher working with Gen Y's was required to demonstrate how the subjects would be utilized in the real world. Students began to have more exposure and grasped the full range of issues and their understanding of the overall needs grew. They even started to become a second teacher in their home. Their philosophy of life was simply to work and produce, leaving no room for any sort of idealism. Their core value system was mainly about Individualism and addiction to work.

Gen Y's students had a better learning platform as they improved their ability to visualize the things that happened around them. A bit of technology became part of their everyday lives. They successfully migrated to the information era. The world required them to be better trained to get a job, as competition was increasing. However, the Gen Y's were labelled as the me-me-me (self-centered) by the times magazine during 2014.

Generation Z

Gen Z: This is the digital age.

Today information is available for free, you can learn anything on YouTube, Udemy etc. It no longer a secret that there has been a digital revolution that has made information free and accessible and that we are living in a societal upheaval, where everything is social. Gen Z's don't care about survival; their grandparents took care of that. They don't care about a decent standard of living either; their parents took care of that. Even the labor does not care about standard of living anymore because even labor has a satellite dish installed in their house. So, if you lower their pay or bind them with a contract, they'll be happy to find another job. Today's students need something else, they want quality of life, not standard of life. Today's workforce is thinking quality of life, which means quality of education, quality of teachers, quality of workplace, quality of job, environment, quality of role, opportunities, learning and rewards and the list is endless.

Now the teachers are dealing with Generation Z students. They are the post-millennial generation and will take the lead in a few decades compared to the previous generation. The intelligence quotient of the student varies in different generations as depicted in the picture above. The Gen Z's possesses high IQ, which may be written as Learning Quotient. They are highly exposed to variety of learning resources available in the market today. The Gen Z's have unlimited resources to understand about the scientific facts. They have access to the globe with the availability of technology devices including smart phones, iPad, chrome books etc. at any time and location.

They are the master of technologies. While they do have a bad reputation to neglect their interpersonal relationships to a greater extent, but they are the ones who voice the social causes in the social media. They are the fast food generations and like to get everything they want instantly, a fact fostered by the instant gratification through digital world in which they are immersed and influenced by youtubers. They have the ability to multi-task, but their attention span is limited.

There is a complete change of attitude. They have demonstrated the ability to take risks to explore and discover innovative products by cross skilling, upskilling, reskilling. These Gen Z's do not require a mere teacher rather a mentor or coach. They need someone, who facilitate them with rich and timely guidance and have a strong debate with them to uplift them to think creatively to solve day to day problems. They expect the teacher coaches to be more friendly, supportive and dynamic in a way that influence them to drive their ideas. What they don't want is a rigid traditional teacher who commands them to get things done which actually dilutes their purpose of learning. It is only those teachers who can better influence these Gen Z's have the caliber to make them deliver results and provide clarity to their purpose of existence.

7

PERSONALIZE YOUR CURRICULUM – THE STUDENT CENTRIC WAY. TIME FOR ACTION

"You can teach a student a lesson for a day; but if you can teach him to learn by creating curiosity, he will continue the learning process as long as he lives." Clay Bedford

7.1 Methods to Enhance Student Engagement

Before pitching to the best practices, I would like to communicate a general notion as well as scientific concept of student engagement. The term carries different meanings to different people. Some identifies student engagement in terms of how actively a student is paying attention to the lesson being taught, raising queries and reflecting his/her understanding by answering teacher's questions. Other defines an engaged student as one who is continuously making eye-contact, gazing on board and seems interesting to lesson being taught. Few may also find a student engaged in the learning process if he/she participates in class enthusiastically with a face expression of everything being understood. Whereas some keep a mere criterion of passing exam as, yes, this student was engaged in class therefore he/she has passed with good grades.

Does it mean that a student sitting on the last bench and on the other corner of the class is not engaged? Does it mean front benchers are most engaged students but student engagement reduces exponentially with increase in teacher-student distance in class? Does it mean that a student who gets an average grade is less engaged than a high scoring student? Or a student who doesn't answers in class is least engaged? How you define student engagement?

Student engagement is combination of cognitive, behavioral and emotional components. And the three components of engagement are inter-related as well as interdependent. Behavioral aspect of student engagement attentiveness in class, attendance, level of concentrations in sessions, engagement with co-curricular activities, peer interaction, collaborations in group assignments, class presentations, etc. Cognitive engagement refers to the individual motivation and self-determination towards learning goals. It also includes a student's personal ownership for his learning achievements and wish for perusing learning goals. Lastly, as the names suggest emotional engagement, it is the aspect of the engagement which internally connects a student to the learning process. It is defined as the level of likeliness and positive feelings of a student towards the learning environment, area of study/subject, people engaged in the process (teacher, peers) as well as overall academic experience.

Generally, the behavioral component is most visible, captured and of interest of different stakeholders in teaching process. It's a contributory factor but it solely doesn't make up the whole student engagement. This component is most assessed, studies and generally remains the area of focus for improving student's engagement with different strategies targeting behaviors related to the concept.

So, as I mentioned that the three components of student engagement are inter-related as well as inter-dependent, you must be wondering that how being a teacher I could affect the emotional and cognitive components. I can take care of attentiveness in class, attendance, and level of concentrations in sessions, engagement with co-curricular activities, peer interaction, collaborations in group assignments, class presentations, etc. but how to make a difference with the emotional and cognitive components?

Methods of enhancing student engagement in classroom or teaching learning environment:

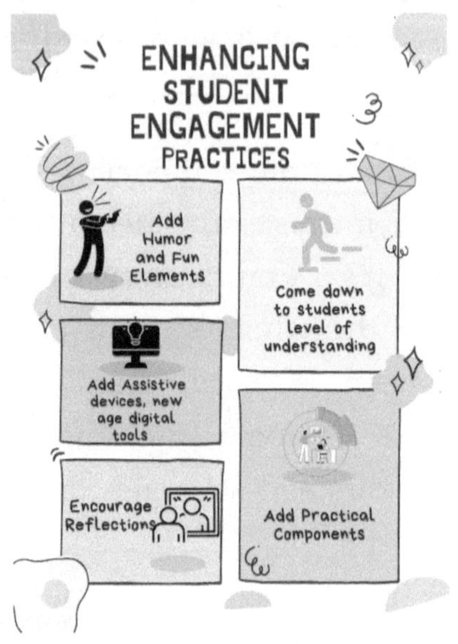

- ***Add humor and fun element***: What most of us do is, enter the class settle students down and bang on to the teaching session. Isn't it? Let's change this habit and add some fun element to our sessions. Let's add some humor, let's add some liveliness to sessions and let's add some spark to our present teaching methodology. To do the same, we can add some fun based real life examples so that learner could relate, we can add some simplified layman vocabulary to describe complex concepts, we can add funny but sophisticated visuals to make the class initially laugh and subtly converge to the topic of the session or interest.

- ***Come to student's level of understanding and kick out the learning hurdles***: Every learner is not a genius but majority of them are average which means that every learner possesses at least a basic capability to understand concepts which are taught to that age group. So, what if a student is not able to understand a concept? Where is the problem? Let's understand from his/her perspective. In order to know their pain-points, we need to get down to their level and reach the core of the problem. Our aim should not be making majority of a class to understand a concept but everyone in a class to understand it. With that mind-set, we have to encourage the discussions around where the problem lies, which point you are not able to understand, pinpoint the concern and here we are.
- ***Add assistive devices and processes to support and enhance the learning goals of the session***: Along with traditional black-board- white board approaches, there is a need to include other assistive devices such as use of flipcharts, group presentations, videos related to topics, role plays, etc. All these make learning environment more interactive and livelier which ultimately raise interest of learners to participate in such sessions.

- ***Encourage reflections***: Call for reflection is beneficial for both teacher as well as a learner. It helps a teacher to understand level of understanding of different learners, pick out mistakes as well as allow learners from each-other as well. Further discussions open up student's mind as well as fill them with confidence. Break-down your session's goals in sub-goals and club those with reflections. Make it a quick round of reflection, individual in case of small classes and group reflections if class strength is high.
- ***Add practical components***: Theory and theory leads to boredom and lack of interest in topic or later may be in subject. So, add some practical components such as role plays, video clips, podcasts, story-telling, class presentations, etc. These processes not only raise attention and interest in subject but also maintain that.

All the above discussed factors enhance student engagement when a teacher applies them with passion and mindfulness. The desired passion and outcome will surface out when a teacher accepts the model of experiential and lively learning.

7.2 Blend Life-Skills into your academics

During my college days, I used to visit Ramakrishna Mutt in Chennai and spend lots of time reading various books on topics that interest me and attend lectures and discourses by various learned swamijis from the mutt. I realized that there are two aspects to education, the objective and the subjective. The objective education is related to the world outside, the subjects and the typical academics type that we learn in schools and colleges, while subjective education is the study of human beings and the self. Our education institutions and most of the teachers today focus only on the objective education as it has measurable results and outcome. There are some teachers who takes interest and bake the subjective elements while imparting the objective education. They are the creative and passionate ones. Infact Swami Vivekananda wanted the healthy blend of these two aspects and I am adding some additional ingredients to the mix. A Career oriented education without character undermines the career itself. Education in its true sense must enrich everyone with ethics and noble values. That is what will improve the quality of life. Teachers are responsible for aiding their students with such skills that will help them succeed in life. There are some who argue that life skills are best learned outside of the classroom which is absolutely incorrect.

Teaching life skills in the classroom will help students succeed both academically and in life. These skills are critical for overcoming school and life challenges. Through the development of life skills, students can learn how to set goals, manage their emotions, handling difficult situations, manage crisis, resolve disputes, budget their time, and make informed decisions. In short, they need to learn how to live and that's something that can't be taught from a textbook alone.

That is why I believe that integrating life skills into the classroom is important.

So how can you incorporate life skills into your classroom? Here are a few ideas:

1. Talk and discuss some facts about failures. I have said it in the chapter 4 of this book that most of the teachers are hard wired to prepare the students for success but are not showing ways to deal with failures. Let us look into 4 valuable lessons that one can learn during failures.

2. Create opportunities that that require students to work together. It can be anything. This is a great way to teach teamwork and communication skills.

3. Hold regular goal-setting and counselling sessions 1x1 with students. In a class of 30 spending 10 minutes with each student over a week is easily doable. You might want to use the OKR's of google in a customized format for students from middle grade. Help your students set realistic goals for themselves, and then help them create a plan for achieving those goals. This will teach them time management and organization skills.

4. Encourage open communication. Create an environment in your classroom where students feel comfortable sharing their thoughts and ideas with you and their classmates. This will help them develop strong communication skills. Insecurity is an emotion that gets easily dissolved when every student in the classroom are emotionally connected. A teacher can easily find ways to make it happen. Just that he/she needs a will to do.

LET US FIRST
Acknowledge
SOME FACTS ON FAILURE

Inevitable

Accept that some failures in life is absolutely inevitable, it is impossible to live without failing at something. It is an integral part of our learning journey

Stressful

You don't get to have a purposeful career raise a family or leave the world in a better place without some stress and discomfort. However each time we do fail and manage to get back up, we not only become a little bit stronger, we tend to learn a little bit about ourselves, the people and situation around us.

Comes with a price

It is during the crisis such as the Covid-19 pandemic that we find the deepest meaning of life. Failure forces us to stop and re-valuate our life. Experiencing and learning from failure is the price one has to pay for the admission to a meaningful and purposeful life.

Teaches us free lessons

The most important lessons in life are learned from failure. Failure teaches us many things about ourselves. We value people, money and relationships only after we have lost them. It teaches us how to survive and makes us be the better version of oneself. As quoted by Elon Musk once, If you are not failing, you are not innovating.

Time management is a critical life skill. By teaching students how to budget their time and prioritize their tasks, they will be better able to handle the demands of school and life.

Organization is another significant life skill. Students must organize their thoughts, materials, and time in order to succeed.

Study skills are essential for academic success. By teaching students effective study habits, they will be better able to retain information and do well on exams.

Preparing for and taking tests is also crucial. Students can boost their academic performance by learning how to prepare for and take tests properly.

7.3 Travel that extra mile to Know your student

All teachers do love their students. However how much one knows about them is the key. With the evolution of this digital wave, we all have heard the term KYC that expands to Know your customer. Whether you open a bank account or apply for a gas connection or a driver license, or ration card, you are supposed to provide detailed information about yourself based on the set guidelines. This need is to better serve them and ensure their identity. Similarly, we got to have something called as Know your Student (KYS), It is not from an identity card or an Aadhar card stand point but getting to know their real identity as shown in the below wheel.

As part of the KYS methodology, one need to understand the five aspects of a student to get to know them completely. Their Belief system, occupation of their caretakers, Financial background, Education level, friend circle, living environment. In other words, knowing the student the life he lives before and after the school. The concept of KYS yields to a stronger emotional bonding with the teacher which has proven effects into the overall well-being of the student.

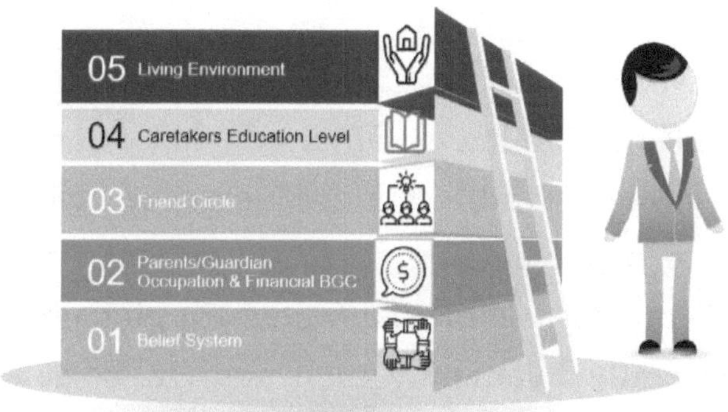

01 Belief System: It is very important to understand the belief system that the student is coming from. It is not his religious background but the belief's he has acquired over the years. It could be based on his several experiences in life that has made his what he is. It is this invisible force that contributes a lot to the behavior of the student. Humans accumulate thousands of beliefs throughout our lifetime, about all aspects of life. We gain them through things that other people say to us, things we hear on the news, things we read, or any other external influences that we are exposed to. Intelligence and culture have developed as a way for human beings to evolve faster more at a mental level. Cultural evolution happens much quicker than biological evolution. Beliefs around effective decision-making, negotiation and business exist in order to help you achieve a certain status in the social hierarchy.

Beliefs around dealing with things like uncertainty and anxiety exist in order to help you maintain mental health and so on and so forth.

In other words, belief systems exist to ensure that the you are capable of fulfilling certain needs that you have, being secure, feeling loved, feeling a sense of belonging, or being able of developing your self-esteem. Most of the time, this process is more like water dripping on a piece of rock constantly. Eventually, the water will be able to shift the shape of the rock, but it will take a long period of time. Sometimes, though, we are thrown into a radically different environment, which exposes us to a completely different way of thinking so suddenly and with so much force that this process can happen very quickly.

This could happen in many different circumstances like joining a new community of people. Reading the works of new and radically different thinkers. Or moving to another country.

Sudden disruptions of a belief system, however, have very strong effects on one's sense of self and one's emotional stability.

02 Parents/Guardians Occupation. Knowing the financial background and the occupation of the student's parents is next. This can help us identify the attention he is getting at home. Parent's attention is the greatest gift to the child. is one of the critical. The routine interactions between the child and parent sets the tone for any societal acceptance and adjustments. Through spending mindful and quality time and energy during the first three critical years of life, parents and caregivers provide their young children with essential experiences that set a stable foundation for future health, social and emotional well-being yielding to academic achievements.

03 Friends Circle. There is an old saying which you will perhaps recollect, "tell me who your friends are, and I will tell you what you are." It has a very deep meaning. A behavior of a student may be judged by the company he keeps. The company influences a lot on the student's characteristic directly on in directly. At that stage of life, it becomes very difficult for the student to differentiate between the right and wrong. They could easily fall prey to the wrong things and invite trouble for themselves. Friendship is a very important bond during our character-building phase. It gives us a feeling of belonging, bring Joy, fun and laughter, lend an extra hand, offer emotional support, and give guidance when you need it. Literally their influence goes well beyond those moments. Infact such deep bonding helps to shape the course of your life. After finishing my graduation, to hunting down my first job while at college, it has made me realize that hard work and perseverance are essential ingredients to getting what you want out of life. They act as boosters to turn your visions into reality. Over the next few years what hit me was the fact that our success and quality of life actually comes down to the people we choose to spend our time with. Questions such as How smart and active you are, how talented you are, the family atmosphere you grew up in etc. does play some vital roles in determining how successful you will be in life. However, the impact of surrounding yourself with people who can lift you higher is way beyond what you can imagine.

You would have seen several examples in our real life where in a person born into riches may lead an unhappy life, while someone from more humble beginnings maybe able to manifest their dreams in record breaking time. This is because of the company they keep, which influences their way of thinking and thus resulting in a mindset for success.

It is proven beyond doubts that our habits determine the person we become. The nurturing environment is an important factor that can have a deep impact on your overall well-being.

If you want to be healthy? surround yourself with healthy people.

If you want to become more confident? surround yourself with confident people.

If you want to get better at teaching? Surround yourself with people who aspires to be so.

We are in the social media arena and it is up to us to utilize it to its full potential and to our advantage. It has become easier to find more like-minded friends across the globe who has similar thinking. In essence, we become more like the people we hang out with.

04 Caretakers Education Level. Research shows that parents or the care takers education level has a significant impact on their children's success. They guide what their kids eat, where they live and even what they wear. They actually influence in a far more effective way. One reason for this strong belief is that parents who are graduates from universities or colleges tend to place a high value on educational attainment. A research published by the National Center for Education Statistics(US United States Education Department) observed the following two insights.

- 45% OF THE STUDENTS WHO ENROLLED IN THE FOUR-YEAR HIGHER STUDIES HAD PARENTS WITH COLLEGE DEGREES AND 26% DID NOT.
- ONE THIRD OF FIRST-GENERATION STUDENTS DROPPED OUT OF COLLEGE AFTER THREE YEARS, COMPARED TO 14% OF THOSE WHOSE PARENTS DID HAVE A DEGREE

The findings of the study suggest that students whose caretakers did not hold a degree but entered the workforce straight out of high school were more likely to believe that a college degree was not worth the cost. They felt they do not need further education to pursue their desired career. I had a personal experience justifying this statement when I went for a career counselling session at an under developed government school in a sub urban district. Upon closely interacting with the 10th grade students I realised that they just wanted to get some job just like their parents, who happen to be daily wage workers. It took multiple sessions to uplift their mindset to understand the importance of education.

One must understand that when you place a high value on educational attainment, it manifests itself in several meaningful ways. For e.g., obtaining certification and degrees, encouraging a strong work ethic and reading more often provides opportunities that are achievement and results-oriented. An outcome of a growing body of a research indicated that a student tends to believe that achievement is to be valued and pursued when their parents/caretakers model achievement-oriented behaviours. It nurtured a strong belief in them to lead to the pursuit of higher learning and successful careers.

05 Living Environment:

There is a direct link between parent's education level and the living environment of the families. According to the National Center for Children in Poverty (NCCP), the less education a parent has, the more likely the family will be considered "low-income." The NCCP study found 86% of children with parents who have less than a high school degree lives in low-income families, compared with 67% of children with parents who does not have a college degree and 31% of children with at least one parent who has some college education.

Another study found that students from a low socioeconomic status affects their family interactions and leads to behaviour problems that in turn affects their academic and intellectual development. Also, parents who struggle financially often creates ruckus in the home which happen to be witnessed by the junior family members. Their inability to deal with depression, low self-esteem is passed on to their children. Students who had expressed difficulties in coping up with various situations are those who have experienced emotional abuse or atleast, have witnessed them in their homes. Hence it becomes very important for the teachers to get to know all these aspects of the students and provide the extra care and nurture to help transform them to be better contributors to the society and be part of the nation's economic development. The world needs education role models and teachers with creative intent who can contribute a lot in achieving this milestone.

Reference: https://degree.lamar.edu/articles

7.4 Divide the batch in byte sizes

In a class of 30-40, it is not easy to concentrate on every learner individually. Every learner has own pace, style and level of grasping concepts. So, I myself do and suggest division of a batch into byte size sub-groups.

What is the purpose of the division?

- ***Collaborating learning:*** Here, the purpose of division is to enables maximum group learning opportunities by means of each other's actions, ideas and values as well as working styles. As everyone has own way of dealing with situation, conceptualizing issues, thinking, reaching conclusion, self-presentation and responding; this byte size grouping will help all the members to learn from each other. When learners will work in groups on assignments, planning, presentations, they will see and grasp that how other members are carrying out that particular process and will consciously or unconsciously imbibe those.

- ***Appreciating diversity***: Along with leaning from group experiences and interactions, learners will also start appreciating other's ideas and will develop a sense of appreciating difference and diversity.

What should be the criterion of the division?

Now, the criterion of division again depends on the motive behind grouping. Are you dividing the batch for a regular class activity, a group presentation or for a particular long-term assignment or for any other pre-defined purposes?

The criterion of the division should be non-academic one i.e., level of activity, personality type, interests, preferences, communication as well as responsiveness levels of learners in the learning environment. This doesn't mean that we are going to club all the evens together, odds together, all the good communicators together or less responsive learners together. But, soon after the identification of preferred criterion of the division, you have to create some approximately homogeneous groups whose compositions would be more or less similar in terms of members' behaviors, abilities, responsiveness level or whichever other criterion you have chosen.

What should be the size of a byte?

First and the foremost which accompany idea of division is what should be the size of each group or what is the preferred size for the same? For a batch of 30 you can divide it into multiple of five as well as that of ten, depending on the purpose of the activity and duration. You can choose to create some permanent groups if you frequently use group activities and presentations, discussions in class or could choose to dissolve group after every activity.

Are we labeling students with division?

The purpose of this grouping is to foster teaching learning process as well as enhanced learning and interaction experiences. This not meant to label or demean any one.

You can give interesting names to groups as per activities or purpose of the grouping. For instance, if you are grouping batch for class activities you can name them as – environment action squad, decoration creative, etc.

7.5 Health and Physical fitness within the classroom

7.5.1 Introduce Classroom aerobics

Physical health is such a factor which contributes to almost every areas of life. Being physically healthy is a boon. We all are aware of the saying 'a healthy mind dwells in a healthy body'. Thus, for overall wellbeing of learners, tutors also hold responsibility to contribute to the physical as well as mental health of learners. Nowadays more and more youngsters are becoming obese, less active, and lethargic and sit with low energy level in classes.

As is a child's body, so is their mind. If they are forced to sit, passive and motionless all day, how on earth do we dare expect their mind to be active, creative and proactive?

Students have to be challenged continuously in the classroom - they have to be moved. Why are virtual games and smart devices so irresistible to children? It is only because these devices are interactive. They let the students decide the path of their discovery. There is no fear of retaliation for every action. They tend to learn a lot from every reaction faced from the device. These virtual games are visually appealing products built on core genetic impulses and operate with subconscious triggers.

Therefore, incorporation of physical activities in classroom in different forms has become more important than ever before. Some of the benefits of including physical activities and movements in classroom are as follows:

- It refreshes the mood and enhances attention levels
- It keeps learners active for longer duration
- It helps to maintain fitness level to some extent
- It encourages individuals to incorporate physical exercise in daily routine

What do I mean by Aerobics in classroom?

Generally, as a teacher or a tutor our focus remains concentrated on lessons and teaching process. But we do forget about the importance of breaks and refreshing activities to recharge/refresh our learners back to the enthusiastic mode. So, here by aerobics I don't mean to transfer whole class/batch to the ground and do a rigorous set of exercise and leaving them tired at last, but

It means small physical exercises say body movements, slight dance moves, yoga pranayama, or anything which you think could refresh the pupil.

Purpose of classroom aerobics

Let's first understand the purpose of the classroom aerobics. Every one of us go through lots of things, varied positive as well as negative experiences throughout the day which affects our level of functioning, mood, enthusiasm to participate in any activity as well as our attention levels. Therefore, the primary aims of the aerobics are firstly improving holistic well-being of the learners and preparing them for lessons with a fresh mindset. Aerobics improves blood flow to all parts of the body including brain, makes feel energetic, enhances concentration levels, etc. Aerobics or similar activities should be prepared for classroom with an objective to make everyone feel light-minded, improve the mood, fill them with more energy and refresh to acquire more concepts.

What all can be done?

As we all know that all groups, classes, batches are different in composition, interests and other aspects. So, being a teacher, you can choose the activities under classroom aerobics as per the individual characteristics of the learning group. You can choose in include mild to moderate level activities or exercise including dance movements, on-spot jogging/jumping/running, stretching exercises, yoga pranayama's such as Brahmari pranayama, eye exercise, light body movements, etc. You can also play light instrumental music, beats etc. The aim of the process is to improve the state of mind, attention level and mood of the learners. Therefore, in classroom aerobics the ultimate goal is the outcome of the activities not the process.

How and when to do it?

Once as per your class/batch's characteristics you have decided the aerobics activities to be included, now comes, who will lead the class or be the in-charge on daily basis. In section 7.4, I emphasized division of batch into byte size groups, which will help in classroom aerobics as well. As now you will be having groups in class so you can use the same to administer classroom aerobics. Everyday a new group member should be given chance to plan and lead the activities; other members of that particular group need to follow the leader. This will add creativity to the aerobics activities as well as will offer a chance to every individual to realize his/her leadership skills, confidence building and sharpen leadership skills.

Frequency/best time

Classroom aerobics activities should be performed before starting of session in the morning and once after lunch as after lunch it starts to feel lazy and most of energy seems drained out. You could also call it as energy breaks or energy booster sessions.

7.5.2. The Breathing Ground for Mindfulness, Calmness and Focus

In present times, increased competition, lack of support systems and rivalry are leading to spectrum of negative emotions among people. Younger generation also didn't leave untouched. As children feel academically pressurized, forced to achieve better and face any other issue in life; those are manifested in the form of anger, aggression, frustration, jealously, even self or harming others behavior and other emotional reactions. Researches have shown that negative emotions affect children's health in many ways. It disturbs the hormonal balance, could lead to anxiety & depression, reduces attention levels, externalizing behaviors (aggression, fighting), withdrawal, etc.

Why breathing techniques in classroom?

Breathing techniques or exercise are the ones which help an individual to relax, calm down, gather attention and lastly focus on a single aspect. At bodily level it helps to improve oxygen supply in body, reduces stress, improve lung's efficiency improves freshness, etc. At mind level breathing exercise enhances calmness, attention and improved concentration levels.

Our ***purpose*** to introduce breathing techniques and exercises in classroom is meant to make the students feel calm and gather focus to grasp new learning in the classrooms. These could be clubbed with aerobics or as individual 5-10 min sessions on daily or weekly basis as per the individual needs and time schedule allows.

Why breathing techniques in classroom?

Now comes what different types of breathing techniques could be incorporated in classroom which are easy to administer under time constraints but are equally beneficial and doesn't compromise on the results of the process. As a teacher or tutor or mentor we are carrying a bigger goal, i.e. holistic well-being of the learners. Thus, in order to enhance overall well-being, attention level and mindset to participate in learning process, we are introducing breathing techniques.

What all breathing techniques can be used in classroom?

Some of the suggestions for easy breathing techniques are as follows:

- *Breathe focus techniques*: In this, one has to sit comfortably and bring awareness to the breathing process. After few shallow breaths try to practice deep breathing and making your belly relaxed. Now, start focusing on breathes with an imagery in mind or phrase (which makes you feel better, relaxed or happy). You can choose to say 'inhaling happiness' and 'exhaling stresses' or anything that makes you feel better.

- *Alternate nostril breathing*: This breathing technique has multiple health benefits for a person; includes relaxation, enhancing of cardiovascular function and lowering of heart rate. In this breathing technique, an individual has to sit in a comfortable position and close one nostril with middle finger and inhale air with the other nostril. Then, the air flow has to be released through the other nostril. This cycle will be repeated for minimum five minutes.
- *Equal breathing*: It is also known as 'sama vritti' in Sanskrit and meant to practice equal length breathing i.e. equal length of inhalation as well as exhalation. One has to take breathe and count up to five and then exhale with the same pace again with the counting of five.
- *Bhramari or humming bee breathing*: it is also called as bhramari pranayama in yoga. It helps to provide instant calmness and soothing in the forehead region. What all one has to do is making humming sound. It could be performed at any place where one feels free to make humming sound. The sound of 'hum' starts soothing the forehead and moves ahead to calm down all sense and provides an extended sense of soothing

throughout the body. It is particularly used to relieve oneself from anxiety, frustration and anger.

- *Deep breathing*: The purpose of deep breathing technique is to inhale more fresh air to feel relaxed and centered. One has to inhale air from nose and hold it till count of 5 and then exhale slowly.
- *Sitali Breathing*: It is another yoga breathing technique which helps to feel the practitioner feel relaxed and also lowers body temperature. It is different from most of the breathing techniques as in these breathing techniques, air is inhaled through mouth but exhaled through nose. In Sitali breathing, one has to inhale air from mouth and hold it a bit longer but not in a forced manner and then breathe out from nose.

7.5.2.1. Mindfulness in Thinking

Nowadays, being stressed, being anxious, and being disturbed with life circumstances are quite common. Most of the time people carry loads of mental burden with them. This load interferes with their present capabilities to perform as well as live the present moment as the load occupies major portion of attention. The same is applicable with teaching learning process. Any sort of burden and continuous thought processing affects attention & concentration, capacity to grasp and sustain information. This situation could be dealt with practice of mindfulness in daily life.

Mindfulness is a mental state in which an individual is fully present in the moment without any other thought process or distraction. The practice of mindfulness enables the student to reduce academic stress & anxiety, regulate emotions and live in the present moment.

How to enhance mindfulness?

- *By practicing breathing exercises*: These exercise helps to focus on breathing and develop a habit of living in present.
- *By practicing guided imagery:* Guided imagery is a type of guided meditation and relaxation technique. It refers to visualization of a place which has a positive association with one's life or an imaginary place which one finds soothing to think of.

To be utmost effective in teaching a tutor needs to be mindful of his/her thought process and able to being present in present moment to deliver the lessons or concepts in an effective manner. Similarly, it's a tutor's responsibility to inculcate the same habit in learners so that they are best benefitted from teaching learning process. The breathing exercise and classroom aerobics contributes to the same.

7.6 Improve the Classroom Climate

Collaborative learning is an important culture enhancer to improve the classroom climate. It refers to the collaborative efforts for learning which includes students, groups, teachers, peer learning, and innovative approach to learning and so on. In order to serve best to our students and yield best out of their hidden potentials, we need to transform our present classroom climate and shift our efforts to collaborative learning approach.

For collaborative learning first, we need to divide our batches or classrooms in groups where the purpose of grouping will be maximizing group learning opportunities by means of each other's actions, ideas and values as well as working styles. Since it is evident that everyone has own way of dealing with situation, conceptualizing issues, thinking, reaching conclusion, self-presentation and responding; thus, grouping will help the members to learn from each other. When learners will work in groups on assignments, planning, presentations, they will see and grasp that how other members are carrying out that particular process and will consciously or unconsciously imbibe those.

The criterion of division and size groups has been already discussed in section 7.4.

Goals of Collaborative learning

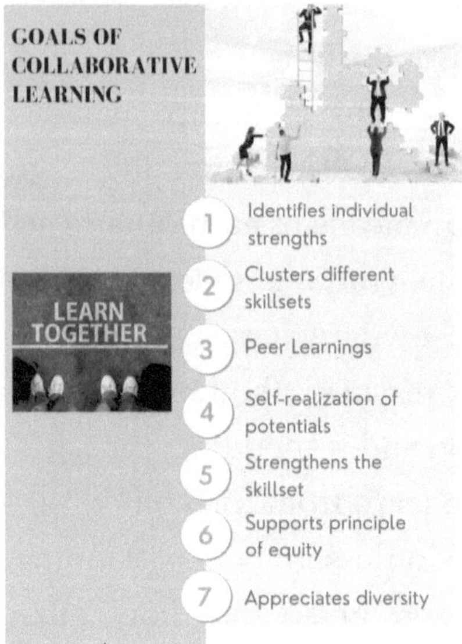

- *Identifying individual strength areas*: The first goals is for the teacher or tutor, in which he/she has to identify the strengths and weaknesses of each learner in the class and then think of placing that leaner in a group to build on strengths as well as diminishing limitations.
- *Clustering different skillsets together*: This goal of collaborative learning is prepared with an aim to create diverse groups with all sort of possible skillsets in a group so that every member is benefitted with such collaboration.
- *Peer learning*: This is one of the primary aims of collaborative learning which allows learners to

grasp different skills, working strategies, working styles from their peer.

- *Self-realization of self-potentials by learners*: Once, the group are in functional mode, subtly the tutor should work on emphasizing the strengths by recognizing, and appreciation those.
- *Strengthening the skillsets*: In collaborative learning process, another major aim of the process is to generate such opportunities that every member of a group gets a chance to portray his/her talents as well as get a fair chance to practice the same.
- *Support with principle of Equity*: Principle of equity says; an individual should be provided support as per the individual need; not same for all. For instance, there are three students in a class who need remedial teaching. All has been sent to remedial class and teacher is providing same lessons to all the three. One child starts to improve whereas other two didn't show any signs of improvements. The reason was teacher was working on spelling rules whereas that was need of only one student, other two were facing problems in grammar and sentence structure. So here teacher went with the principle of equality whereas principle of equity was more appropriate to apply.

- Appreciating diversity among groups: Within collaborative learning, students are able to see the similarities as well as differences in the skillsets, approaches towards problems and solutions, thinking patterns etc. Thus, help to develop a culture of understanding others and supporting which ultimately leads to appreciating diversity.

7.6.1. The four -ION's in collaborative learning

Here, I am presenting an approach to Collaborative learning. It could be easily used under different classroom setting in order to achieve goals of collaborative learning. The model has been designed with holistic approach to learning i.e. life skills development, practical skills development and not merely including the academic aspects or based on academic processes.

As per this approach there are four steps in the process of collaborative learning.

1. Exclusion: First of all, a teacher needs to identify the strengths and weaknesses of learners on non-academic grounds. So, what should be the baseline for the exclusion in this first step? For instance, communication skills, leadership skills, specific arts or cooking or any other skillset could be used as a baseline to carry out this process. This part of the process could be considered as first 1-2 month of academic session.

2. Separation: Once the criterion for exclusion has been decided, now it's time to segregate the class into small groups. Here the demand is to create heterogeneous groups i.e. group members should possess strengths in different areas. For instance, there is no meaning of making a group of all the leaders, artists or others together. This is so; because, such groups will be homogeneous in nature. There will be less opportunities of learning and growth of members of such groups since all of them possess more or less similar skills set. In spite of that, the groups should be heterogonous in nature, say one member with exceptional leadership skills, one with artistic mindset, some may be good with writing whereas others with decoration, etc. This part of the process could be understood as initial 2-5 months of an academic session.

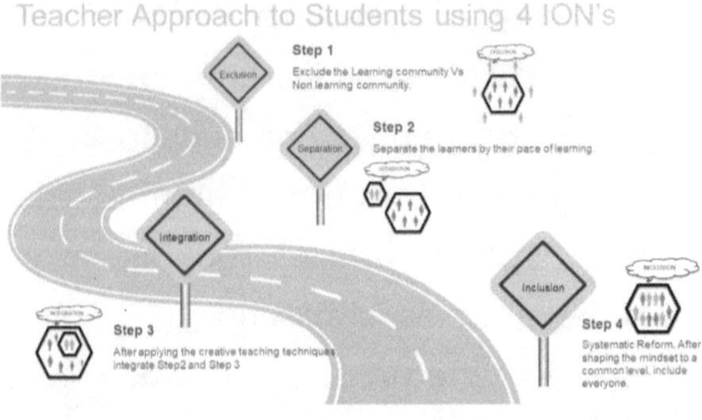

3. Integration: By now the groups have learnt to work together, became aware of each other's strengths, skills and also learnt a great deal from inter-personal interactions. It's time to merge the byte size groups into a single batch same as before exclusion. The purpose of integration is to reunite the sub-groups into the group, create a sense of belongingness to group, neutralizes ego & thought processes and develop appreciation for diversity. Here, it is responsibility of a tutor is foster acceptance, respect and mutual understanding among group members. By the end of the integration process students must accept, appreciate and support each other in respect to their strengths and weaknesses.

4. Inclusion: It is the last step which includes acceptance, appreciation and support of fellows and group members at mental level as well. Thus, in inclusion, all the members of the group really start accepting each other and extend genuine appreciation and support as and if needed. For instance, in the movie "Chakde India", the coach got a very difficult team and all the members were from different places, though all were talented and deserving. The coach faced great difficulty in resolving internal issues and creating a sense of belongingness, internal support and appreciation which lastly helped them to win.

The team was integrated by the selection committee whereas that was only at physical level or at superficial level whereas there was no connect among the team members. Therefore, integration could be understood as 'we feeling at physical/superficial level' whereas inclusion as 'we feeling at mental level'. As a whole, lastly the ultimate goal of the process is to segregate the group in sub-groups to create opportunities for customized learning and lastly merging the sub-groups into one to foster acceptance, support and appreciation of diversity.

Integration and inclusion collectively could make up second half of an academic session.

7.6.2. Enhance Classroom Ambience

To build a learning school, we need to first build a better classroom. We all know one's imagination has no bounds. If I ask you to close your eyes and imagine a classroom of your dream, what would be your blueprint. Let us start with this exercise. Assign this task to all of your students in small batches.

Reports from credible sources have proven that a design of a classroom affects children's learning. Research has confirmed the positive impact factors such as lighting, air quality, sitting postures, color choices and innovative designs.

Consequently, changing our environment can be a very powerful way of improving our well-being, behavior and performance. The key is to fully understand which changes will have the most positive effect.

According to a report from University of Salford, the differences in physical characteristics can explain up to 16 per cent variation in learning progress over a year.

The first apprehension that comes to one's mind is the investment to create such an environment. In my interactions with teachers who were behind some the most creative classroom acknowledged that many of the improvements were made to their learning spaces with very little cost. Small changes can go a long way. Simple modifications to classroom layout, wall colors, display designs and more can significantly impact learning development and achievement.

It is proven beyond doubt that the arrangement of desks, benches and the ambience of the classroom contributes to the development of creative learning and teaching.

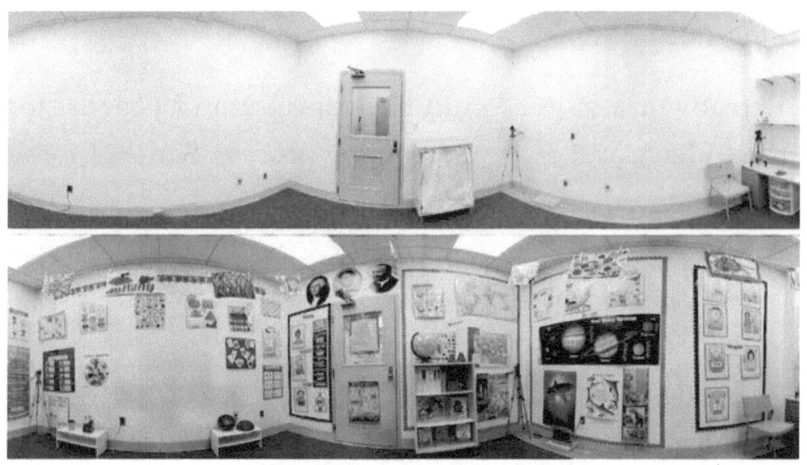

Pic Source (NYTimes - BY MICHAEL GONCHAR)

Importance of creative classroom

A creative classroom is the one which displays talents of students; side-by-side sparks innovative thinking. It offers an opportunity to learn with fun and search for related information. A creative classroom doesn't mean overly decorated bright and distracting place, but it should be a display of art pieces and ideas of the students. It could also include planned display of certain piece of information for learning or break out activity purpose. These initiatives can have a major impact on students' mental health and well-being. Research has shown that learning environments that are comfortable and welcoming can have a significant impact on learning outcomes. These initiatives can be as simple as changing the color of a classroom or creating a student group that welcomes everyone.

Importance

A creative classroom could have spectrum of benefits for the students and teaching learning process. Some of those are as follows:

- A creative classroom could act as an idea Pandora of ideas which could spark innovation in student's mind and direct actions.
- A creative classroom could encourage students to walk an extra mile and think out of box. Thus, enhances thinking ability and leads to innovative mindsets.
- A creative classroom could give a sense of belongingness as well as self-responsibility as that it maintained by collective efforts of all.
- It gives freedom of expression by means of art pieces and thoughts displayed on boards and classroom walls.

By building a learning school I mean that every aspect of the school or particularly individual classrooms should be decorated by the students. It will serve dual purpose. Firstly, when students will develop and place their ideas, art pieces and decorations on the wall; it will generate a stronger sense of belongingness as they themselves have contributed something to it. Secondly, it will develop them think innovatively and get some ideas from others works as well.

The creative classroom should be mandatory as it will allow students to portray their talent. The decoration and student's contribution to classroom should be dynamic. It means the decoration, art pieces on the wall and in corner of the classroom should keep changing. It will keep the classroom atmosphere lively and may lead to sprouting of different ideas in the learner's mind.

7.6.3. Create an atmosphere of Joy

According to research, providing a joyful learning environment is key to student success. While it seems self-evident that happy students learn better, it's important to remember that this belief is backed by science as well. Having fun in class by playing a game, watching a funny video, or working as a team to complete a challenge, can be valuable and ultimately help us create the type of classroom we all want to be in. Regardless of a teacher's style, joy is critical for success.

I believe that creating a learning environment in which teachers with diverse philosophies and classroom management styles are welcome is an important part of cultivating joyful learning environments. In these environments, teachers can infuse daily doses of silliness.

Student's learning is hindered when emotions cloud their judgement. Students who experience fear, pressure, low self-esteem, or anger are unable to generate new ideas and cannot learn optimally if emotions interfere with their learning.

According to neuroscientist Martha Burns (2012) there is chemical called dopamine that plays a role in regulating the brain's pleasure and reward circuits. When dopamine is released, it triggers an intrinsic reward system. Humor can increase the retention of knowledge and decrease stress, as well as increase resilience, if it is incorporated into curriculum. Teachers can use humor to engage students and keep their attention, thus making the environment more inviting. Of course, humor also helps to make the classroom environment more inviting in general.

An important aspect of creating an atmosphere of Joy in your classroom is to have students take ownership of their learning. When students feel like their learning is something that is meaningful to them, it will be more likely to stick in their minds and make an impact on their lives long after they leave your classroom. Additionally, it's important to have students feel like they are having an active role in the learning process, not just sitting and listening to facts being repeated to them.

Activities like role-playing, story-telling, and art can be used to help the little ones connect with their learning. Kids learn best when they have a lot of hands-on activities and it is important to keep the classroom environment fun. Organizing games and competitions, as well as field trips, can also help boost attendance and engagement levels.

7.6.4. Find Open Space for Learning that complements the classroom

When a school is developed with a view to stimulate learning, the infrastructure and the environment can function effectively as the third teacher. What primarily initiates the learning is the relationship that the student has with the teacher, parent and environment. The need for open learning spaces evolved due to the changing trends in the education sector. Skills such as creativity, innovation and collaboration are the key skills required to survive in the job market today.

A traditional classroom is a more teacher-centric way of delivering academics and adheres to a specific format. Open learning spaces have a more student-centric approach; wherein the teacher functions more as a coach and allows students to learn according to their individual tastes. Open learning spaces is known to foster development of creativity and motivate students to solve problems in a collaborative manner.

(ILETC) research from the University of Melbourne suggests that deep learning and student fulfilment are most likely to occur in diversified learning activities and innovative learning spaces. This highlights the fact that a school should have a variety of learning spaces and open learning spaces should complement traditional classrooms.

The vision and the school's philosophy are the building blocks on which the educational activities are determined in a school. At the same time, the teacher can also plan the environment where she will conduct an educational activity. Matching the educational activity with the appropriate space where it can be conducted is key towards understanding how learning spaces can be effectively designed and used. A Tinkering Lab is an example of a learning space that supports the practical. Teachers guide the students to learn as per their individual differences' creation of an idea. It is an ideal environment to implement the design thinking approach right from the beginning-from defining the problem for ideation, creating a prototype to rigorously testing the prototype. Deciding the key learning spaces is based on the learning objectives, which have been defined by the leadership team. Collaborative interdisciplinary projects are planned by the technical team designated for the innovation lab along with the facilitators that combine knowledge skills, techniques, and materials for both digital and product design.

Activities at the innovation lab are aligned with the curriculum and can be measured with the learning objective. Concepts in the innovation lab are based on the philosophy of hands-on learning through building solutions and prototypes.

(The above narrative is an extract from a news article authored by principal, Chaman Bhartiya School)

7.6.5. Eliminate the Mimetic desire and get'em out of the rat race

According to Rene Girard, humans have a sub-conscious desire of imitation to others. And this is evident under many circumstances as well. You might have seen children playing in park who want to play on the same swing where another child is playing or every child want to have a same balloon which other child is having. They want to have it because they have a mimetic desire to imitate; it's not their conscious thought process but a sort of following behavior because someone else is having that. Students tend to choose what majority of the folks are choosing without really knowing if that works for them.

The same happens in studies, subject selection as well as stream selection. A student wants to go for biology because his best friend or an intelligent student of the class is choosing that subject. The particular student doesn't have own conscious will to study biology but choosing the subject either as a conforming behavior or just with mimetic desire to do so.

How this mimetic desire could be eliminated? How learners could be supported to take more informed and future oriented decisions? Why a learner is unconsciously trying to choose a subject or follow someone else? Why he is not following his/her own strengths, ambition and interest areas? Why so? The possible reasons I could come up with are: there is a possibility of non-realization of own interest areas and potential, no one might have ever emphasized the strength areas and may be a learner never took some of his/her skillsets seriously. Yes, these could be the possible reasons.

Being a teacher or tutor, most of our attention is focused around academic areas and skills as those are generally considered as the parameters of success in life. In order to widen a teacher's vision, I would like to introduce a well-known and established model of intelligences in the field of psychology. The model has gained wide popularity worldwide and also getting acceptance in Indian education system these days. It is 'multiple intelligences model' by Howard Gardner.

Multiple Intelligences Model

According to this model everyone is intelligent in his/her own way as well as have different proportions of all types of intelligence in them. According to Howard Gardner, every individual differs in possession of the different types of intelligence and there is a primary or dominant intelligence(s) in everyone. This is one of the major reasons of individual difference in classroom that every learner understands, performs and learns differently. Everyone has his/her own capacity and have their own pace of learning. Considering those varieties of intelligences, it can be said that there is no stupid learner in a classroom. Understanding the role of multiple intelligences in general as well as in education domain will help a tutor or teacher to widen their views on teaching methodology, incorporating variety of innovative teaching techniques and going creative in approach to make the diverse group learn better, which earlier seems homogeneous. Teachers have to be more of facilitators, observers, and lesson designers in such situations. Since children like to play and have fun, the learning and teaching process should be suited with the nature of the children themselves.

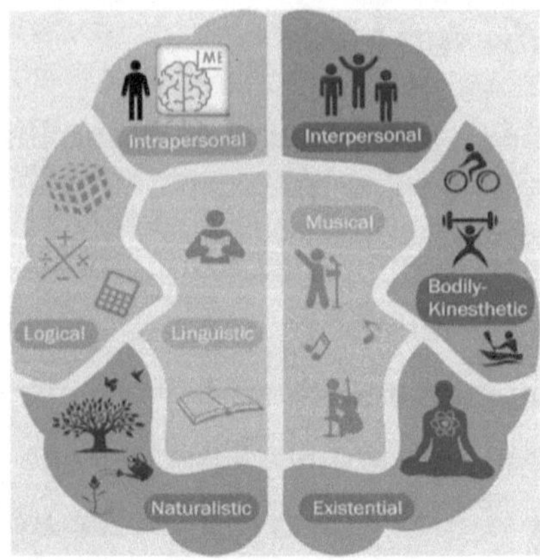

According to Multiple Intelligences model, there are nine different types of intelligences. These are:

Verbal-Linguistic Intelligence: This Intelligence deals with verbal and linguistic abilities of an individual means individuals high on this intelligence are good with words and use of language with fluency both in verbal and written form. These individuals are also categorized as 'word-smart'. These individuals are good in writing, memorizing verbal information, etc.

Characteristics of individuals with high Verbal- Linguistic intelligence:

- They are good in reading and writing
- They are able to explain things well
- They are good at remembering written and spoken information

Mathematical-Logical Intelligence: This intelligence is related to reasoning and logical analysis of situations. So, individuals high on this intelligence are good at reasoning, logical analysis of situations and recognizing patterns, etc. They are well able to establish link among numerical concepts, deduce out patterns and establishing relationships, etc. These are generally known as 'number or math smart'.

Characteristics of individuals with high Mathematical-Logical Intelligence:

- They are good in abstract thinking and enjoys the same
- They are more capable of solving complex computations
- They possess excellent problem-solving skills

Musical Intelligence: This type of intelligence includes an enthusiasm for music, rhythm, beats, signing and music creation. Individuals with high musical intelligence manifests likeliness for musical beats, they like to tap, hum, create and copy music & beats as well as interested in learning musical instruments, dance and music creation activities.

Characteristics of individuals with high Musical Intelligence:

- They recognize and remember music melodies and beats easily
- They enjoy singing and playing music
- They have a deep understanding or zeal to learn musical structures and melodies

Visual-Spatial Intelligence: This intelligence deals with processing of visual information. Individuals with high visual spatial intelligence are good in visualizing objects, direction, etc. in their minds. They are good in reading maps, drawing, sketching, etc. At times these individuals are also called as 'space smart'.

Characteristics of individuals with high Visual-Spatial Intelligence:

- They are good in solving puzzles
- They easily recognize patterns
- They enjoy activities and subjects like visual arts, drawing, craft, painting, etc.

Bodily-Kinesthetic Intelligence: It is an ability of an individual to control bodily movements and handling objects skillfully. Individuals good at this intelligence are outstanding in performing bodily movements & actions as well as in physically controlling objects. These individuals are also called as 'body smart'.

Characteristics of individuals with high Bodily-Kinesthetic Intelligence:

- They possess excellent physical coordination
- They are remembering things by doing
- They are likes activities like sports and dance as well as enjoy creating things by their hands

Interpersonal Intelligence: This intelligence covers an individual's abilities to deal with people, group reciprocate appropriately and maintain interpersonal relationships.

Characteristics of individuals with high Interpersonal Intelligence:

- They are able to establish and maintain long-term interpersonal relations.
- They are good at conflict resolution in groups
- They communicate well

Intrapersonal Intelligence: This intelligence deals with an individual's ability to of being aware of self; such as emotional state, own feelings, motivations, desires, etc. Individuals good at this intelligence are highly self-aware, able to regulate their emotions, self-analysis and reflections, etc.

Characteristics of individuals with high Intrapersonal Intelligence:

- They possess high level of self-awareness
- They are able to analyze their strengths and weaknesses well.
- They understand the basis of their feelings and motivations.

Naturalist Intelligence: Individuals high on this type of intelligence are interested in environment, learning about other life forms, exploring environment, etc.

Characteristics of individuals with high Naturalistic Intelligence:

- They are good at relating to nature
- They enjoy topics related to environment
- They enjoy outdoor activities in natural climates, exploring environment, etc.

Existential Intelligence: This intelligence is quite different from other intelligences proposed by Gardner. This intelligence is associated with higher life goals, deep realizations of existence and meaning of life. It deals with questions such as why do we take birth, why do we die, what is the meaning of life? Etc.

Characteristics of individuals with high Existential existence:

- They are seeking information on meaning of existence.

Application in classroom

By understanding the model of multiple intelligences, a tutor or teacher could understand the meaning and need to focus on skills other than merely academics. Also, a tutor could choose to plan activities or lesson plans to make it appealing for learners with different type of intelligences and learning styles.

How to eliminate the mimetic desire?

Here are few steps utilizing which a tutor could head towards elimination of mimetic desire of students regarding choice of subjects and interest areas at large.

1. *Identification of strengths area*: Firstly, you as a tutor are responsible for identification of interest areas of the learners you are teaching. Remember, we discussed the creation of byte sized groups in earlier section. For grouping we already need to identify strengths and weaknesses of learners.

Thus, along with group creation, focused group discussions, your classroom observations, interpersonal skills of learners and Know your student method could be used to identify the strengths.

2. *Realization of strength areas to learners*: Once the strength areas have been identified by the tutor, it's his/her responsibility to communicate the same to the learners in order to make them realize their strengths and feel more competent. Thus, a tutor need can use appreciation, rewards, open recognitions, etc. to make learners realize their potential as well as enforcing them to work on those areas as well as take some steps to strengthen weak areas.
3. *Encouraging for pursuance of strength and interest areas*: Next step taken by a tutor should be encouraging learners to excel in their strength areas and pursue their interest. Number of researches has proved that individuals who chose careers according to their strength and interest are more successful in comparison to their counterparts. Therefore, a tutor should create such opportunities that every individual is able to practice and sharpen his/her skills in the classroom as well as assign such activities that could practice the same skills in real world scenario.

4. *Mimetic desire eliminated*: As learners will become aware of their strengths and interest areas; they will be less likely to follow others blindly. Now onwards, they will chase their own passion.

7.6.6. The 6 I Approach

6 I approach refers to a combination of six elements named as Interest, Intuition, Ideas, Initiative, Implementation and Innovation. I have developed this approach with my more than a decade teaching and training experience. I would like to share this with you as well, as I believe that it will help tutors to make their teaching more effective and influential. By using this approach, a tutor could evoke a new wave and enthusiasm in learning.

Interest: It is the foremost requirement of any learning process. If there is interest, an individual will put efforts, search for more information and will remain involved in the process with enthusiasm. On the other hand, if an individual lacks interest in a topic or a subject; he/she could not bring out best of his/her potential. Thus, foremost responsibility of a tutor is to evoke interest in a topic or subject or the learning goal of a session.

Intuition & Idea: Once a learner becomes interested in a topic or idea, he/she will start thinking about that and will eventually come up with new thoughts or ideas or solution related to the same. This is the point where innovation starts.

Initiative: Once an idea is conceived, now an individual start taking actions in relation to the idea. He/she starts taking new steps to work on the idea which has emerged out of the interest and intuition. At this point, social factors come into play. At times an individual may feel restrained to take certain steps to move towards the goals as those are bounded by certain social factors such as gender, socio-economic status, etc.

Implement: Here implementation refers to researching out more information related to the conceived idea. In this, an individual research for more and more information related to the idea and tries to consolidate his/her learning or bring out something novel.

Innovative: All the above steps of approach lead to innovation in terms of findings as well as learning process.

Basically, this approach reveals a process by which a tutor could spark interest in learners in relation to any topic of novel area which could or could not be related to academics. Thus, a tutor holds both responsibility as well as opportunity to inculcate a sense of exploration and push to go an extra mile, in students.

7.6.7. Super Mario Effect in the Classroom

According to Mark Rober, an individual succeeds in life or in any area of life, if he/she keeps learning and reframes situations in order to achieve the ultimate goal. Rober conducted an online study and found that the group which was given reward on performance stayed motivated and tried to achieve higher. On the other hand, the other group which was not given any reward lost motivation and dropped out after one to two stages of the game. Thus, he concluded that reward was the motivating factor which anchored the rewarded group to go further even after several failures as reward was having a positive effect in the situation.

According to him, if failures are taken in positive ways and an individual keeps a focus on the learning path without giving up, he/she will achieve the goal. The Super-Mario Effect has various implications in real life situations, academics and other fields.

Implication of Super-Mario Effect in teaching-learning process:

When learners focus on the prize or goal, the process ultimately becomes lighter and interesting to them. It asks a learner to learn and gain some insight from failures but focus specifically on those; which means that a learner should grasp from the loopholes in the last process which lead to failure but should not fix on failures as that will lead to negative thought processes. The failures and challenges make the process of growth and learning more interesting.

How teacher/tutor could incorporate Super-Mario Effect in their teaching processes?

Super Mario effect can be applied to foster learning motivation and experiences among learners. Just a simple step of introducing a 'reward system' could yield mind-blowing changes in learner's classroom behavior, motivation level as well as overt performance efforts and finally changed classroom dynamics.

What should be rewarded?

As we are teaching generation Z learners and the world is continuously evolving, we need to go creative in rewarding as well. So, the criterion of reward should include but not limited to academic performance; extends its horizons to appreciation of hobbies, interests, noble ideas, creative efforts, divergent thinking initiatives to name few. As every learner is different, each one of them has a unique set of skills and everyone deserves appreciation.

Thus, a tutor/teacher's classroom reward system should include possibly all sort of skills/abilities/interest to be appreciated so that every individual feel acknowledged this motivated. The rewards should be reasonable (no need to reward each and every effort but something innovative or different than usual), appealing (a reward should be age and interest appropriate) and variable (it should keep changing as well as include variety of reward to be appealing to diverse classroom).

How to go different?

Reward system is quite common in lower classes starting from kindergarten, but as standard advances, it seems to lose importance. But it is not the case. Several studies have revealed that use of reward system keep students motivated and improve their holistic performance in classroom. Prizes, appraisal, grades and money are some of the general rewards. But, being a tutor, using non-monetary rewards could be a better fit.

Being a Z-generation tutor, one has to think different. So here are some "different reward systems" which could be introduced in classrooms:

- *Star/Pearl of the week/month:* One of the most appealing and interesting reward for students is when they see their names on display board. It motivates as well as empowers them. One could choose to have multiple boards or spaces to acknowledge students with different skillset say academic- co-curricular etc. This will give multiple stars / pearls rather than just one; motivating number to students to see themselves on that place.

- *Individualized mentoring opportunity*: This could be appealing to students of higher grades as at that level student seeks for guidance and mentor who could lead them to better professions and study areas.
- *Prize wheel*: It comes under monetary reward. A tutor can choose this system along with others or solely. This system could work better if the prizes are already known to students. The best performers as per their hierarchy i.e. first, second and third could be given an opportunity to spin the wheel and try to get the desired prize over there.
- *Offer special responsibility*: Students generally feels important when a tutor / teacher offer them some special responsibility in classroom or some related activities.
- *Display of art-piece with remarks*: Suppose a student has prepared a mind-blowing art piece, or won a dance competition; a tutor could put that art piece or award ceremony's photograph on the class display board (with a reasonable note / remark) as a reward to make child feel appreciated and boost his / her motivation to such better acts or produce art pieces in future as well.
- *A handwritten card to parents*: It a moment of pride for both a child and a parent when they receive a positive remark from school or institution where

the child studies. And if it is customized, then it will definitely go in life-time achievement collection. Thus, a handwritten card from teacher to parent worth to be a strong reward.

Other than the above suggested reward and reward systems, a tutor could choose to brainstorm and come up with something innovative, search on internet as well as researches to bring out a best fit reward system as per the composition of learning group or classroom interest areas.

7.6.8. Regular Break out activities

These are the fun and real-life oriented practical activities meant for improving group dynamics, communication and cohesion among groups and team members.

Some of the other purposes of breakout activities are:

- Enhancing networking in groups
- Improving communication skills of group members as well as level of communication
- Improving public speaking skills
- Improving presentation skills
- Improving self-presentation
- Reducing hesitation in presenting self in group and in social situations

Frequency of Break-Out activities

Use of breakdown activities depends on the purpose of learning sessions or targeting skill. A breakout activity could be used on daily/weekly/monthly basis as resources and time allows.

What type of activities could be included?

There is no specific activity to serve the purpose of breakout objectives but any activity which seems relevant to your goal behind the activity could be the best fit. Thus, a best breakout activity is one which helps to achieve the purpose of the session. For instance, simply class decoration could be a breakout activity, a debate, an outdoor activity, ask-me-anything, etc. could be used.

Benefit of use of breakout activities

- Breakout activities lighten the environment
- Breakout activities provides a base to central idea of sessions
- Breakout activities enhances group cohesion and communication levels

7.7. Classroom Edutainment

Although, edutainment is a new word but it's not a new concept. It refers to use of entertainment-based materials such as videos contents, games, TV show clips, podcasts, etc. for educational purposes. The use of entertainment-based material to serve learning goal plays a crucial role in the learning process as it lightens the concepts, present ideas in realistic manner as well as adds a fun element to learning. It basically utilizes modern electronic devices, software as well as platforms to for education purposes.

Most people are distracted in this generation. they are distracted while at work, they are distracted when they are with their friend circle and family members, while performing their morning routine, during intake of food, while commuting to school/college. They just are comfortable in getting on the rate race every single day with no purpose. Most people just don't care enough about any efforts in their personal development and growth. Entertainment is more important. Most people have replaced their life achievements and goals with TV, Party and social media. Their life is characterized by entertainment and disruption, not learning and creation. This results in feeling disconnected from relationships. They get stuck in the jobs they hate and their life is on the fast track to disappointment and they end up in state of confusion. If you don't want to keep your life in mediocrity focus on learning and creation and introduce the new subject of edutainment to help students handle such distractions and provide a platform to enjoy their learning journey.

Researches has proven that use of multiple methodologies and incorporation of appealing components such as audios, videos, learning games and so on, makes learning a fun and appealing to learners. It ultimately affects the learning outcomes positively. It enhances personalized learning, visualization as well as creativity in the learning process.

7.7.1. Develop a culture of thinking. Visual Thinking

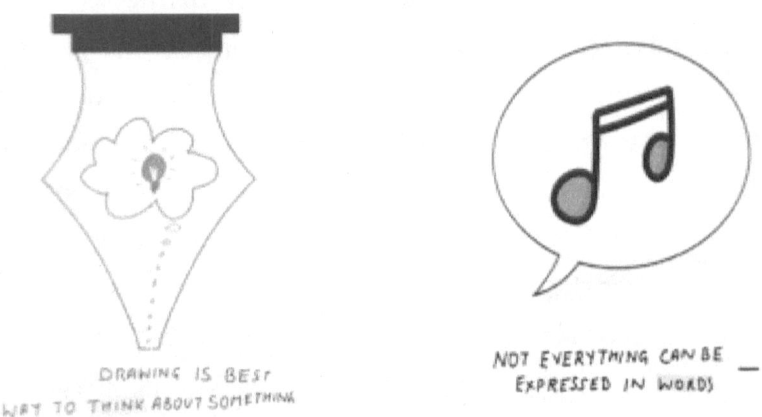

Picture Courtesy - @Doodlevoice

Imagination is the key! In the recent years there has been an enormous interest in every matter that has something to do with the brain, as seen in the popularity of brain apps, books and games. For generations rote learning has been our principal way of remembering things, with repetition the sole focus of our memorization. A more effective way of remembering, though, is to use our imagination. Rather than repeat information over and over again we can create highly imaginative visual stories to connect with what is to be remembered. Aside from being fun, remembering made-up stories engages our brain in many more ways than traditional memorization. Words are processed on one side of the brain, images on the other. Repeating words is ineffective, but creating images from those words is incredibly strong.

Use of diagrams, graphs and charts are conventional methods of teaching but you may wonder about the reason. These all are visual representation of verbal data which is easy to comprehend and remember. On the same line, there is another concept called 'visual thinking'. The phenomenon and practice enable people to think of verbal data and concepts in form of visual or pictorial form in their minds which makes it easy for them to understand even complex concepts.

How often have you seen people go back to reread sentences in books because they felt they missed something or could have understood something better. It happens a lot. Contrastingly, how often you find people watching a movie and would rewind every few minutes to make sure they don't miss anything. Chances are none. The reason is because the movie engages us visually. We watch the screen play, the body language, we feel the emotion and be in that moment till the end. Reading the text is different. I wish there was an 'encoding' process that transforms the text into images for us to truly understand. We need to create the experience. It doesn't mean that watching something is better than reading. It just means that using visual processes to trigger your imagination helps us remember things better. Reading text can also trigger the imagination far beyond what we see on a movie screen. It is the use of imagination that will give you a better mind and memory to learn faster and better. That is the power of visuals. Harnessing meaningful opportunities is a crucial part to creating a culture of thinking in a classroom. The prime vehicles for propelling learning in classrooms lie in the opportunities that teachers create. If planned properly, opportunities can be engaging, thought-provoking, and fun for students.

What is visual thinking?

Visual thinking is a phenomenon through which people understands concepts, ideas and information through visual processing. It empowers an individual to understand things around him/her in form of series of pictures and it yields more powerful learning experiences which carries longer durability in comparison to verbal learning experiences.

Your capacity to remember doesn't have to diminish with age as long as you relate the concepts, ideas and information through visuals. In fact, by using a little imagination, you can train yourself to recall the most obscure details.

Visual thinking strategies (VTS)

VTS is a specific learning approach which was developed by Abigail Housen. It is a teaching method; an art piece or picture is used to initiate a discussion. The teacher is only the facilitator who appreciates different viewpoints and validates individual views whereas students direct the discussion by their ideas, thoughts, inputs, critical analysis of each other's perspectives, reason out and listen attentively. The group is responsible for interpretation of the art piece shown and develops critical thinking skills.

A tutor could choose to use VTS in different sessions as per need to induce the habit of visual thinking and analysis.

Role of visual thinking in learning process

Visual thinking plays crucial role in different areas of life including teaching-learning process. Thus, here are some of the importance and reasons to foster visual thinking in learners.

- Visual thinking stimulates creative side of the brain which also enhances the way an individual looks at normal things around him/her thus come up with more novel and creative ideas.
- The purpose of improving visual thinking in learners is to empower them to present their

thoughts, ideas and experiences in visual form which is easy to understand for everyone.

- Visual thinking enhances critical thinking and problem-solving skills.
- It increases learner's memory of learnt and understood concepts.

As a tutor, your aim should be to include more and more visual inputs in your teaching process which will help the students to interact with and interpret visual information at regular basis. This will enhance their ability to understand as well as present their own ideas in the same form with ease such as presentation of ideas as mind maps, graphical organization of information and so on.

As a whole being a tutor, it is an important responsibility to improve learner's visual thinking skills in order to make them more competent to visualize the world in a more creative manner.

Learners, Visual Vocabulary & Sketch noting:

Visual Vocabulary: It refers to a dictionary of pictures which is prepared in an individual's mind with cluster of certain themes but not in alphabetical order. For instance, the pictures or sketches of fruits will be clustered under one theme whereas all the vehicles related pictures or sketches will be stored at one place in mind. With continuous application of visual thinking strategies in classroom and teaching sessions, visual vocabulary as well as confidence to use that also increases. Visual vocabulary is a pre-requisite for sketch-noting.

Sketch notes: As soon as learners starts thinking in visual form i.e., in the form of picture and other visuals, they start to apply those in their study as well as other learning process. They start making visual notes which are generally known as sketch notes. Sketch notes are a combination of sketches and supporting text to capture a key idea of a session or lesson. Thus, a learner summarizes his/her learning in form of sketch notes which could be later referred for revisions.

For e.g. Try to draw this below picture and caption it. Test it with your friends, you can see many different responses and that is exactly the beauty of sketches. The imagination is limitless. It makes you feel very good under any stressful situations. Infact you can make visuals out of your own stress factors and craft a story out of it.

My caption for the first pic will be "Sharing of ideas" and second is "one cannot chase happiness as it is never found outside". Please write your captions in my website or my email id specified in the starting pages.

Finally, there's communicating your story to others. Make strong impressions articulating your ideas, below is what tried to draw. It is a simple road map with milestones. Now you might want to try one, list down all the next six-month milestones you would want to accomplish and express them through a simple road map. You don't have to be an artist at all to jot them. I feel I can quote myself as the best example. I always believed that I can never draw as I am not inclined towards it since childhood. However, the belief changed when I started expressing ideas through such simple drawings.

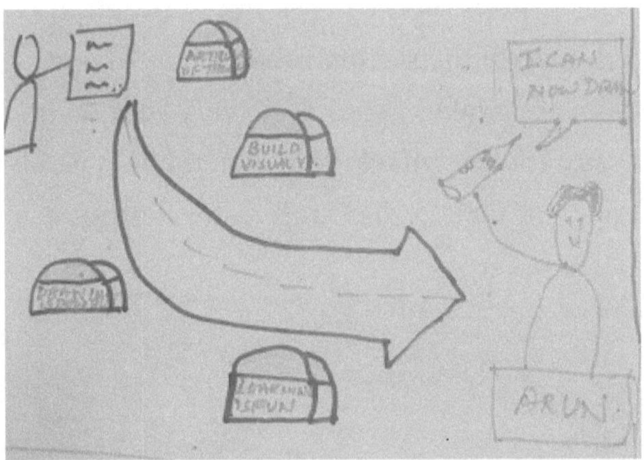

Now look at the below picture that shared from few of my batch mates who attended the visual thinking class last year along with me. I don't remember the name but all credit to him to express the thoughts on an un used plug point. He/She will be happy to see this being referenced as part of my book.

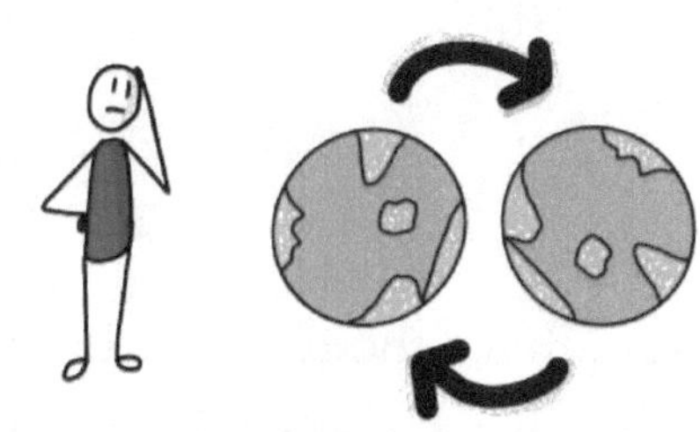

Now try this one. Below three pictures that represents a famous proverb. Give it a try and guess it. This was part of the assignment from the visual thinking workshop and below is what I came up with. If you can guess it, I will continue with my drawings otherwise, I will not attempt it any more 😊

When we sleep, that's the time our brain consolidates our memory, so anything you've learnt during the day is consolidated into stronger traces in the brain when you sleep.

Keeping your mind active is as important as exercise to the body is reading and with consistent practices of visual thinking activities will keep your mind sharp, helps you to stay creative and keeps your mind active on a task. Train yourself this unique skill and pass it along to your students and am sure they will cherish the learning for the life time.

The Googlification Mentality – A critical thinking killer

Sometimes to get the information we are searching for involves a creative sense. If we shut that sense, not only we will struggle for getting the right information but also the entire process will make us look stupid. Here is a typical real-life incident on this subject. The second part of the narrative is taken from a blog of my post graduate class mate and with her consensus, I included it as part of my book.

It was the time of Diwali - the festival of lights celebrated widely in every part of India, and my family were busy decorating the house and arranging the lamps, calling friends, preparing for the fireworks. After few hours, the lights were lit in our apartment complex and the time for fireworks started. Every one of the friends and the family stepped outside. It was simply a treat to watch. After a couple of hours, one of the kids mistimed the rocket. It changed its direction and hit the dress of my friend. Fortunately, it was not a major accident. However, the incident that I wanted to quote here is how two mindsets of people from different generation who witnessed this episode responded. The first thing that the newer generation set of folks did was executed command to google. "Hey Google, what to do during a burn injury?", "Hey Siri, what is the immediate care to be provided when you experience a burn" asked my friends nine-year-old son. While the old-generation folks including the resident security, was already there in front of them armed with cold water, ice cubes, tooth paste, cotton cloths, asking them to soak it and wash it off with cold water. I am sure we all have had those moments where we just can't remember a restaurant that we might have visited n number of times, a movie, or a name while we were hanging out with our friends and that just drives us crazy and we end up googling it. The digital generation of students are so dependent on an google algorithm that we are failing to use our critical thinking? Does this mean that all these Google's, Siri's and Alexas's are making us lazy and stupid?

There is no harm in using the facility available but the pertinent question is at what cost? Teachers need to impose these thought process to students who are so much reliant on technology. At the beginning of the internet revolution, I remember Google was incapable of sourcing even a simple movie name which I was trying to recollect as part of a memory game that I was playing with my friends. That was the time when the number of searches on Google was somewhere around 18 million and today the number of searches is more than 3.7 billion a day. In that more than 60% of searches comes from mobile devices. This data itself was provided to me by google. Sound's interesting right?

A high school teacher is giving an assignment: "Does the U.S need a New Constitution, should there be a change to the Preamble of the Constitution?", the first thing the students did was Google the question- type in word for word and look for answers. You walk into a 3rd grade classroom, it's not any classroom, it's a Google Classroom, you will see smart boards and children busy swiping, and posting their work. These kids post their work on See Saw and the classroom looks like an Internet Cafe/ Starbucks. The formative years of these children are spent on apps, smartphones- digital world, and it not only molds the person in how they access this information, but also how they visualize, conceptualize- Information is always accessible- there by eliminating the process of critical thinking. Students today resort to a binary- credible or not credible, where the answer becomes the be all and end all and is more independent. Educators are finding it difficult to "Google Proof" the assignments.

I go to a gathering, I see many friendly debates, arguments that would have turned into an active engaging dialogue/conversation, die out prematurely, when participants reach out to Google, to end the argument.

By habit, most people look at the first few results, and without even validating its accuracy or credibility, end the discussion and the whole conversation runs out of steam. Instead, if we would let two people just debate the topic, the conversation would turn into listening and responding, opens up new perspectives, and you would get to know the person a bit more and have a social connection, instead of just shooting the argument down by googling.

This was the dotcom boom era, trying to resolve an error code, I looked it up, and I still remember, a co-worker giving me that condescending look that signified a sign of defeat that I was incapable of thinking like a programmer and reached out to google it. Today, I look at every young millennial around me, and wonder "Are they a better googler or a better programmer". Googling is no longer a sign of weakness, but the first step towards finding a solution. Why would I memorize something, when I can look it up? Train your brain to know how and where to look for information instead of recalling the information.

Google is an Integral Part of our Life

I saw this sign board on a hospital wall. As much we have gotten more exposure and awareness of medical conditions with Google and technology, people in the Medical Profession cringe with the amount of questions we ask, or the diagnosis we public do, by cramming the brain with pieces of disconnected information.

Today we live in a world, where we can divide the demographics of the people as B.G and A.G(before and after google). Look at the different ways Google is influencing our day to day life: You go to Gmail, its recommending a reply for us, you use Maps, its suggesting restaurants, places of interests along the way, I am getting news story suggestions based on what my interests are, Google suggests what I should watch, where I should go, what I should eat- it's shaping my thinking process, filling in the gaps, it's becoming a passive aggressive cognitive tool at my fingertips. It really does feel like we have outsourced our thinking capability to Google.

We have to understand and accept that Google is an extension of our collective memory. B.G, we had to store information in our brain, because it's a lot of effort and time to look it up again. Our brain stores information in a hierarchical format, things we learn from all sources was constantly mixed with new information we gain. That's how learning worked and it was not necessarily efficient, because, we do lose some old information when we update with new. But our phrasal learning, allows actively putting information in a correlated fashion, brewing up new ideas and thoughts- this manipulation of information remained a key aspect to our creativity and imagination. It made us understand things deeply. Information at our fingertips, although is super liberating, and more convenient, is making us more and more reliant on external memory for our everyday living. We search and look up exactly what we need and we obtain it in microseconds. Google is an index-driven medium. If we approached a book by looking at the index, would we get the full picture of the book, would we know what the book was all about? That's how I view this. We should rather start thinking, how to mold and condition the brain to process the information that we obtain from those indices and derive meaningful outcomes.

"We become what we behold. We shape our tools and then our tools shape us" — Marshall McLuhan when he rephrased Winston Churchill's, "We shape our buildings and they shape us".

Our brains are fascinating, they adapt quite easily. In a world where social connectedness is at the peak, there is no stopping our brains to be digital friendly. We cannot fight the technological developments, but rather embrace it. We need to hone our skills to make sense of the mass curation of the data in front of us. It's not that our brain is lazy, but Google is faster! There is no proven research yet on the effect of tools like Google on our critical or logical thinking abilities. Bottomline, use the Googlification as your last measure in your search of knowledge or information. You can use your critical thinking skills to leverage google and not use google in a way that compromises your critical thinking.

7.7.2. Order-takers to initiators

Pic source Vectorstock – 18012063, @DoodleVoice

What is the purpose of our teaching and in-general learning we impart to a child or a student or any learner? Are we giving skills and creative mindsets to our students and children to think out of box or just giving them guidelines and structures to follow? Are we giving them the sparking point in order to research further and understand concepts on their or just filling their minds with well-cooked lessons?

This is where the question comes that whether we are raising order takers or initiators? In order to analyze this, let's first understand what I mean by order-takers and initiators. Order takers are the one who follows instructions, works well with structured environment, accepts facts as presented to them, not use-to with innovation and divergent thinking; these sooner or later develops into rote learners and well-confined within thinking boundaries. It is not their fault actually but the approach taken to teach and raise them led to this outcome. So, order-takers basically grows into responders, who work as per demand or need but either not habitual or refrain from taking initiatives on their own. On the other hand, initiators are the one who are use-to with think widely, fact checking before acceptance, ask questions; try to apply concept, etc. They are also result of the approach taken to teach and raise them. In both the cases, hereditary factors can't be denied.

Both looks perfectly similar, but what differentiates them is their approach towards learning and later then consolidates into way of life. What all required to raise initiators in first accepting the model by a teacher himself or herself and then manifest the same in ideas and behavior.

Here are some steps whose successful implementation could lead to development of initiator demeanor in learners.

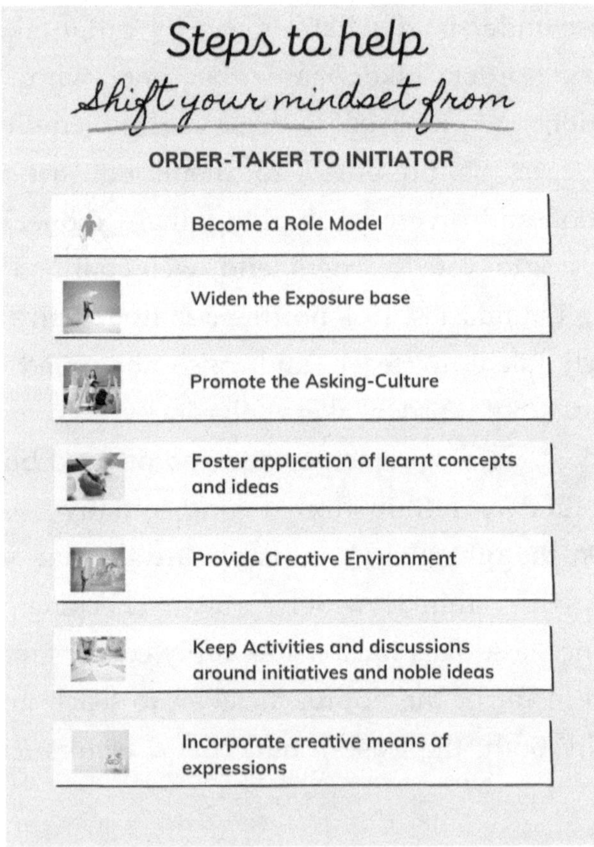

- ***Become a role model***: Before you initiate the process of developing initiators in your classroom, you need to portray the same behavior. Its human tendency that he learns by acts of others as that is overt and easy to grasp.

- ***Widen the exposure base***: Try to introduce more novel, different, activities and concepts, in correlation to the present concept. It will generate interest in the present concept being discussed or taught as well as will learners will relate that with present. You can also choose to introduce some new out of the context idea if you feel that holds an importance to the learners. Here you can either choose to just introduce a concept and leave the spark so that class could themselves research and come up with information and other aspect. Or you could choose to accompany the idea with an instant discussion.
- ***Promote 'the asking culture':*** Some of us like a quite well-mannered class whereas others chose a short question-answer session at the end of sessions. In order to raise initiator spirit, we have to promote 'the asking culture' in the class. It will lead to
- ***Foster application of learnt concepts and ideas-*** Generally once a concept learnt is either revised before a test or a final exam. Does it really make a sense? Is that the only means of learning? To go and imprint everything in the exam manuscript and later your learning will be reflected in the exam scorecard. Actually, a big no!!! We need to

build a habit of application of learnt concepts in real life. We have to build that mindset in learners that whatever you are learning is applicable in real life and therefore it has been included in your curriculum. You need to demonstrate different uses of same concept across contexts as well as different application of same objects, gadgets, techniques. Once this idea of multiple applications will settle down in learner's minds, they will themselves try to experiment, test and learn from their own experiences.

- ***Provide creative environment***: You can also choose to place some posters, pictures, charts, drawings and info-graphics in the classrooms to indirectly attract the attention of the learners and compel them to think, research and ask about those. It will foster divergent thinking. For this, you can choose to bit vague and creative in approach so that learner will not get direct clues but they have dive deep to grasp those ideas; rest depends on the age of learners as well as understanding level as well.
- ***Keep activities and discussions around initiatives and noble ideas:*** Keep a regular daily or weekly slot for discussions about what personal interest areas of student which could range anywhere from cooking, arts to mechanics. Give them an open forum to express their ideas and get deeper

insight by means of input from more experienced and experts in those areas. For this, you choose to call or arrange some experts from the field, if the resources allow.

- ***Incorporate creative means of expressions***: Give chance to open and creative expressions. Researches have proven that creative expression provides a path to internal and unconscious thoughts to surface out and eventually enter into conscious minds. So, by providing such opportunities, you will allow learners to come up with new ideas as well as a space to present their ideas which could otherwise left buried. The means of expression could be verbal, written (poems, writing pieces), arts, crafts, and many more.

7.7.3. Introduce Video-making and Podcasting as a way of learning

Most of the tutors prefer books, written materials, presentations and classroom discussion as primary choice of teaching learning methodologies. Some of which are conventional methods whereas some are newly adopted, all assisting the teaching processes. But nowadays, videos and podcasts are new normal in teaching as well as in other related processes. These enhance liveliness in sessions, sparks interests, initiate discussions and make a session more effective. Where video is simply a recorded moving picture file, a podcast is a digital audio or video file which is present on internet and different websites which could be downloaded and listened by anyone.

Introduction of video making and podcast in teaching sessions will help to achieve better learning goals as well as to spark enthusiasm & high attention levels.

7.7.4. Add public speaking and story-telling as a way to develop personalities

In general, goal of curriculums, lesson plans and teaching sessions are highly focused around teaching-learning process. What all matters most of the times is the understanding of concepts, application of same and lastly grades achieved with that learning.

But teaching Z-generation is evolving day by day. Nowadays the horizons of teaching process are widening, including more and more areas of a student life. One such area which is targeting with teaching side-by-side is personality development of learners.

Personality is not something which develops overnight but it's a lifelong process. But being a teacher and spending a fairly large amount of time with students, we teachers use to have an impression on their personality whether intentionally or not.

With intentional perspective of personality development, we can add public speaking opportunities and storytelling sessions as means of grooming our student's personality. In order to achieve the same, it is crucial to understand the role of these two processes on different aspects of personality of an individual.

How public speaking and story-telling enhances personality of an individual?

- First of all, it helps to improve self confidence in relation to presentation of thoughts in a social setting. It is foremost benefit of the public speaking practices.
- It helps to build social relations.
- It helps to improve inter-personal communication skills including making appropriate eye-contact with audience, maintaining appropriate voice tone and modifying the same across different situations.
- It helps in perspective taking as well as handling criticism which is a crucial part of social as well as personal life in general.
- Practicing public speaking improves active listening and reciprocation accordingly.

7.8. Ignite Interest in the subject

Tutors always take a pride on good or outstanding result of the result of our batches isn't it? A tutor puts tremendous efforts to deal with diversity in the classroom and make everyone understand the concept to his best. So, the pride is must. But, is it solely a tutor's effort to teach which brings out the results and learner's understanding of concepts? Yes, to a great extent but not solely. One of the major determinants is a learner's interest in the concept or the subject which compels him/her to go an extra mile to take a deep dive into it and explore more.

Does a learner already carry the interest to learn or it could be generated as well? Yes, off course, interest in a particular subject or concept could be ignited? What all needed is a proactive approach by a tutor and a right method do achieve the same.

Some of the strategies discussed in this chapter such as use of break-out activities, 6-I approach, use of multiple-intelligences model and creative classroom building can successfully help a tutor to achieve this goal.

7.8.1. Use Feynman technique

"The more a learner focuses on the meaning of the information being presented, the more elaborately he or she will process the information" John Medina.

Teaching is hard, anybody who has tried the profession can confirm that it can be tough to keep monotonous material engaging. This means you have to help kids figure out what information is important for them to pay attention to; their curiosity can get lost in a sea of facts.

The Feynman Technique is the perfect and very creative technique to learn something new, to help deepen your understanding of a concept, enhancing your recall of certain ideas, or reviewing for tests. In other words, if you are able to explain a complex concept in simple terms, you have a good understanding of the concept at hand. Doing this will also help you recognize your problem areas or areas of confusion, because this will be where you either get stuck when explaining the concept or where you have to resort to using complex terminology.

Have you ever tried explaining your job or what you do to a 1st grader student? Common give it a try right now as you read this line. Once you frame your thoughts around this, you then try to explain the same to a sixth grader then to a twelfth grader then to a college graduate, then to a working professional and finally to an eighty-year-old person.

Were you able to crack it by this simple exercise. Did you feel that "Ahaa" moment? The Feynman Technique is all about giving yourself that Ahaa moment when you finally put all the pieces together to understand something by explaining the same to different categories of people.

This mental model was named after the Nobel prize-winning physicist Richard Feynman, who was recognized as someone who could clearly explain complex topics in a way that everybody—even those without degrees in the sciences—could understand. He was able to take the mystery out of complex scientific principles. Feynman was also named "The Smartest Man in the World" by *Omni* magazine in 1979.

What this methodology is not?

This is not the methodology to use if you are trying to memorize something. This is also not a technique to use on concepts that you already find to be simple or easy to understand.

Feynman technique in teaching:

A tutor must incorporate Feynman technique in teaching process; it will boost the teaching outcomes. As Feynman technique involves getting down to the learner's level and explaining a concept to him/her in the simplest possible way, it makes everyone in a batch to understand a concept clearly. Firstly, a tutor has to prepare himself to deal the variance in the class. Thus, utilizing this technique, a tutor could effectively deal with the diverse learner's pool in a batch.

Using the Feynman Technique allows you to apply the concepts that you learn to real-world problems it gives a platform to grasp the concepts of complex understanding. It helps to improve your teaching skills holistically as you are essentially trying to teach yourself the fundamentals of a subject. This overall enhances your critical thinking skills about a particular topic or subject.

Students and Teachers:

Students can utilize the technique to better understand their lessons and concepts in groups. Another way to make an effective use of the technique in teaching-learning process is to assign higher class students to teach some concepts to lower grade students. As the higher-grade students will prepare to tech lower grade students, they will themselves clarify the concepts step-by-step. This will help them to explain concepts in simplified manner. This will allow them to practice and master the technique, clarifying their own concepts in depth; develop confidence, practice teaching as well as presentation skills.

Example: Suppose you have to describe psychology profession to a farmer. Here, you decided to go by Feynman technique to achieve this goal.

To a Farmer: Generally, majority of farmers are illiterate and not much aware of world outside their villages and farming. So, you came across such a farmer and told him that you are a psychologist. Now, the farmer asked what does that mean, what do a psychologist do? You told him 'Sometimes when your farm production is not up to mark or you become worried about that, you feel stressed'; a psychologist study why does it happen and how to help such people feel better'. Thus, you simplified a complex concept to a farmer in layman terms and without use of any technical term as well as relating same to his real-life experience.

I have personally experienced that analogies are the best way to simplify a concept that is complicated. Analogies are the foundation of learning from experience, and they work because they make use of your brain's natural inclination to match patterns and create insights out of them.

Analogies influences a lot on what you perceive and remember. It helps you associate it with things you already know more easily and processes any new or unfamiliar information creatively.

One example of an analogy created by Feynman encapsulates the power of his technique. He was able to take a question regarding human existence and simplify it into a simple sentence that even a middle-schooler could understand.

Explaining these concepts to your fellow colleagues will not only stimulate your senses, but will also provoke emotional responses that help you retain the information.

You might want to do a quick self-assessment. Without referencing your notes for the next day class, go through all of the information that you are trying to learn and see for yourself how far you can get in explaining the concepts without getting stuck. The beauty of this technique forces you to completely understand a concept without which you wouldn't be able to explain it to a child. In this way, the information is written in your memory as if it is written on a stone. It just remains there for-ever.

As you are able to grasp ideas and concepts quickly, no matter how complex they are, your academic performance will definitely show an improvement. By constantly practicing the Feynman Technique, you will be able to develop good learning habits that will improve the effectiveness of the time you spend hitting the books.

7.8.2. Elevator Pitch technique

Young kids can't remember anything they see or do in the morning or even a few minutes ago. Everyday, students spend hours getting lectured by teachers and spilling their guts out on homework. Wouldn't it be better if we could use that same time to teach them how not to get lost in the wind?

This is a discussion about a new approach to utilize the hidden power of mind to retain a particular information called as "The Elevator Pitch". The Elevator Pitch is simply the ability to summarize what you are studying or what project you are taking on in under 30 seconds, so that it's easy for anyone to understand without having the time and attention to give your project their full attention. This method can transform the way we teach our students and prepare them for the real world ahead. In other words, an elevator pitch or elevator speech is a short description of an idea or a topic that explains the concept in a way such that any listener can understand it in a short period of time.

An elevator pitch is meant to last the duration of an elevator ride, which can vary in length from approximately thirty seconds to two minutes. Therefore, the main focus of an elevator pitch should be making it short and direct. You may find that as a refined extension of the Feynman technique with a shorter duration. This challenges the students into thinking how to reduce the time and words to still convey the same message or the subject of discussion.

You give a topic of discussion to your students. It can be subject topic or any non-subject topic. Give them the time to prepare and help them in their preparation. Then make them deliver the same in their own little ways and again make them deliver it in a shorter duration.

Once you master at this art, create a platform for demonstration with the school/college leadership and you can see how it helps you personally in your career journey. At the same time, it will equally be satisfying for you to see the joyfulness in the learning process.

7.8.3. Connect the dots Technique

Researchers have shown that group activity increases the learning potential of the students. Connect the dots is one such group activity. Here you assign all topics from the same chapter of the subject book. Each student will pick up a topic and at the time of presentation, they will need identify the predecessor and successor topic connect them to do the presentations or write up if it is a writing activity. You develop the empathy skills here as the students not only think and prepare the topics that are assigned to them rather they will need to discuss, think and connect the topics from others to make it meaningful. It can be articulated in graphical, visual drawing or plain text format.

8

SHORT TEACHER-STUDENT STORIES THAT INSPIRES

"Better than a thousand days of diligent study is one day with a great teacher"

Story 1 – Mrs. Bhatt's approach towards her student John brought back his interest.

It was a typical day in Mrs. Bhat's third grade classroom. The students were working on their individualized math worksheets while she circulated the room, offering help and encouragement. She noticed one student, John, who was staring off into space and not working on his assignment. Mrs. Bhat sat down next to John and asked him what was wrong. John told her that he was having trouble with the work and didn't know how to do it. Mrs. Bhat looked at the worksheet and saw that it was a review of addition and subtraction facts. She knew that John was capable of doing the work, but he was just struggling at the moment. Mrs. Bhat thought for a moment and then had an idea. She asked John if he would like to help her teach the other students about addition and subtraction. John's eyes lit up and he nodded eagerly. For the next few minutes, Mrs. Bhat and John worked together to come up with a plan. John would stand up in front of the class and explain what he had been struggling with. Then he would teach the other students a strategy for solving the problems. When John was finished teaching, the other students were clapping and cheering. They were so proud of him! John had found his confidence and felt proud of himself too. This was just one example of how Mrs. Bhat was able to engage her students and help them learn in a way that was fun and meaningful. She always looked for opportunities to individualize instruction and make learning relevant to her students' lives. As a result, her students loved coming to school and were always excited to learn

Story 2 – How Mr. Nandkishore extended his support to a troublesome student.

It was another busy day at school and all the students were eagerly working on their assignments. Mr. Nandkishore, the teacher was walking around the classroom, lending a helping hand where needed. He was always so patient and kind, and the students loved him dearly. But there was one student, Vikram who was proving to be a challenge. He was disruptive, constantly talking out of turn and refusing to do his work. Mr. Nandkishore had tried everything he could think of, but nothing seemed to help. Then, one day, he had an idea. Instead of getting angry with the student or scolding him, he decided to try something different. He asked him to stay after class for a few minutes. When the other students had left, he sat down with Vikram and asked him about his life outside of school. It turned out that he was going through a tough time at home and was feeling really lost and alone. Mr. Nandkishore listened patiently, offering words of encouragement and wisdom. He told him that he was valuable and that he had so much to offer the world. By the time the conversation was over, Vikram has a completely different outlook. He was calmer, more focused, and determined to do his best. Mr. Nandkishore had found the key to unlocking this student's potential. From then on, he made a point to connect with him on a personal level, and he went on to become one of his most successful students.

Story 3 – The story telling approach of Mrs. Saunders to her students created better engagement in learning

It was creative thinking that led Mrs. Saunders to become a teacher in the first place. As a child, she had always loved learning new things and coming up with new ways to do things. Her own children were grown and out of the house, and she found herself with more time on her hands than she knew what to do with. So, when she heard about an opening for a kindergarten teacher at the local school, she decided to apply. Mrs. Saunders quickly found that she loved teaching. She loved the challenge of finding new and interesting ways to teach her students the things they needed to know. And her students loved her for it. They loved the way she made learning fun. One of the things that Mrs. Saunders was known for was her storytelling. She would often use stories to teach her students important lessons. And she always made sure to add a little bit of creativity into her stories. As a result, her students would often be so engaged in the story that they would forget that they were learning. One day, Mrs. Saunders was telling her students a story about a princess who was kidnapped by a dragon. The princess was very scared, but she was also very brave. She didn't give up, even when the dragon seemed to have her trapped. Suddenly, one of the students raised his hand. "Mrs. Saunders, how did the princess know what to do?" he asked. Mrs. Saunders smiled. "That's a very good question," she said. "And the answer is that the princess used her creativity. She thought of a way to escape that the dragon never would have expected. And that's what saved her." The student nodded, and Mrs. Saunders could see the wheels turning in his head. She knew that he would never forget this lesson. And she was right. Creativity is something that Mrs. Saunders continues to instill in her students to this day. And she knows that, because of her, they will go on to do great things in their lives

Story – 4 The Compassion of Mrs. Divya uplifted her student's morale.

It was a dark and stormy afternoon. All students were busy preparing for the skit in the evening school function. Mrs. Divya was Jimmy's class teacher in the previous year. She was nowhere connected to his current grades. Her compassion drew Jimmy and all of her old students, towards her since beginning. Mrs. Divya was grading papers in her classroom, when she heard a knock at the door. It was one of her students, Jimmy. He looked scared and he was soaking wet. "Ma'am, can I come in?" he asked. "Of course, Jimmy. What's wrong?" "My uncle has come to pick me up. He informed my mom is sick. Looks like she can't come and see my skit tonight. I'm feeling bad." Mrs. Divya's heart went out to Jimmy. She knew how much he was looking forward to see his mom watch his skit. "Jimmy, I'll tell you what. I'll go to your skit tonight. I will help your mom watch it live. " Jimmy's face lit up. "Thank you, Ma'am!" That night, Mrs. Divya went to Jimmy's skit, published the event live through YouTube. He was so happy to see her there. The next morning, he came up to her and said, "Thank you so much. You made my night." You not only came to support me in my skit but also helped my mom watch it live. Mrs. Divya was happy that she could help Jimmy in his time of need. She knew that this was just one of the many ways she could better engage her students.

Story – 5 Story of how Mr. Raman created a team spirit to uplift an upset student.

It was a sunny day, and the kids were outside playing. Raman, the science teacher, was inside, grading papers. He heard a commotion and went to the window to see what was going on. The kids were gathered around Ankitha, who was crying. Raman went outside to see what was wrong. "What's going on here?" he asked. "Ankitha's mom is sick, and she's really upset," one of the kids said. "I'm so sorry, Ankitha," Raman said. "Why don't you come inside and we'll talk about it." So Ankitha came inside, and Raman sat down with her. He asked Ankitha about her mom and what was going on. Ankitha told him everything. "It sounds like you're feeling really sad and scared," Raman said. "Yeah," Ankitha said, tears welling up in her eyes. "It's okay to feel that way," Raman said. "Myself and all of your friends are here for you". And then Raman did something really amazing. He took out a piece of paper and started drawing a picture. "This is your mom," he said. "She's in the hospital right now, but she's going to be okay." As Raman continued to talk, Ankitha started to feel better. The other kids came in and sat with them, and they all talked about their moms. Raman had a really special way of reaching his students. He was always there for them, no matter what. He listened to their problems and helped them find solutions. He was a true gift to his classroom.

Story – 6 Story of how Ms. Smitha helped her student find her courage.

It was the first day of school and the teacher, Ms. Smitha, was eager to get to know her students. She started by going around the room and asking everyone their name and what they liked to do for fun. When she got to the last student, a shy girl named Sarah, she asked her the same question. Sarah quietly mumbled her name and then said, "I don't know, I've never really had any friends." Ms. Smitha's heart sank when she heard this. She knew what it was like to feel alone and she didn't want Sarah to feel that way. So, she started to include her in games during recess and make sure to sit with her at lunch. She even invited her over to her house to play. Sarah slowly started to come out of her shell and by the end of the year, she was one of the most popular students in the class. Ms. Smitha was so proud of Sarah and she was glad that she was able to help her find her courage.

Story – 7 Story of a teacher encouraging a student to giving it back to the society.

There was once a teacher who had a student that was truly special. Not only did this student have an amazing gift for learning, but he also had a heart of gold. The teacher just couldn't help but notice all of the good that this student was doing in the community. One day, the teacher decided to bring up the subject of giving back to the community. He told his student about all of the ways that he could help out, and how important it was to do something that was meaningful. The student was so inspired by what the teacher had said that he knew just what he had to do. The student started by organizing a food drive for the homeless shelter. He made posters and flyers and handed out copies everywhere he went. Within a few weeks, they had collected enough food to feed hundreds of people. Then, he got involved with Habitat for Humanity. He started helping with construction projects and donated a lot of materials and manpower. He even helped build a house himself! The student's tireless efforts brought happiness to everyone he touched. His teachers were amazed at his compassion and his kindness, and they knew that they would always be grateful to him for bringing light into their lives.

Story – 8 An important lesson from Ms. Ross about patience.

At first, it was difficult for Ms. Ross to get the attention of her class. They were too busy playing games or goofing off. But she persisted, and over time, her students started to listen to her. Ms. Ross was determined to teach them everything she knew, and she knew a lot—she had been a teacher for many years. One day, Ms. Ross was teaching her students about patience.

She explained that it was important to have patience because it took time to learn something new. She then shared an example of how patience had helped her learn about calculus. Calculus is a difficult subject, and it can be difficult to understand. However, Ms. Ross had patience, and she was willing to learn the subject in order to help her students learn it too. She was patient, and she persevered. Eventually, she was able to help her students understand calculus, and they were able to learn it too. Ms. Ross's story is an example of how persistence can pay off in the long run. Her story shows us that if we are willing to work hard, we can achieve our goals. Her story also teaches us that it is important to have patience, because it takes time to learn new things.

Story – 9 Story of an angry student and the approach of a teacher

A young student was always in a bad mood. No matter how much effort his teacher put into teaching, nothing seemed to make a difference. One day, the student came into school angry and hostile. His teacher tried to talk to him, but the student was unresponsive. That afternoon, the student came into the Teacher's Room with a sad look on his face. He had realized that he was in a bad mood because he was angry at everyone and everything. The Teacher told him that it was okay to be angry, but that he needed to take it out on something else instead of letting it build up inside him. The student agreed and promised to try to control his anger from then on.

Story – 10 How Mrs. Nithya's approach to a shy kid helped the student immensely.

A shy student walked into Mrs. Nithya's classroom on the first day of school. The room was already half full of students, and the noise level was high. The student was so shy that he couldn't even speak to the teacher. Mrs. Nithya didn't waste any time. She went over to the student, pulled him into a hug, and said, "It's going to be okay. I'm here to help you." The student felt a sudden burst of courage and started to speak. In fact, he couldn't stop talking for the rest of the day. The teacher helped the student learn how to control his voice, how to be vocal without being loud, and how to communicate with other students. The student started to feel more comfortable in class, and eventually he became one of the most outgoing students in the class.

9

TEACHER ARTICLES FROM MY NEWSPAPER COLLECTION

I have the habit of collecting articles that related to my area of interest. Of course, teaching is one of them. There is no better way to stay updated with the latest research and facts than reading inspiring articles on teaching. Furthermore, such articles will also help you in your journey to becoming a better teacher. In this section, I have compiled some of the articles on teaching from my endless collection. You too can read them for information, learn from their examples, or use them as a reference for future teaching assignments. Reading research articles also helps you to stay up to date with the latest trends in your field.

Pic: iStock

A learning ground

Learning at school comes with its own advantages and experts tell us how it improves a child's psychological, social, and physical development

Respedit.Chennai
@timesgroup.com

A school is not just a place for learning. It plays a key role in the overall development of a child. According to educators, if higher education is a medium to acquire a degree, school education is essential for an all-round development as it shapes one's personality, thoughts, and grooms the cognitive abilities too. Besides imparting knowledge, it helps in developing the young minds on three aspects.

PSYCHOLOGICAL ASPECT
When a child is born, his or her mind is like clay. School plays a major role in moulding and giving it a perfect shape by developing *the thought process in kids. Educators in school* also

an inclusive environment. "I believe that children's growth should be parallel to the nation's development as they are the ones that will lead the country in future. And here, school education brings a sea of change in one's life. It stimulates curiosity in young minds and improves the thought process. It plays a key role in moulding a nation's future by facilitating all round development of its future citizens," says educationist Vikram G.

SOCIAL ASPECT
Parents and immediate family members are the only people the child has human interactions with when they learn to talk. However, school is the first avenue of socialising for a child. The place serves as a platform to befriend other children while interactions with teachers and other staff help them develop their social skills. Also, children imbibe various sociable practices such as empathy, friendship, participation, and the habit of helping others at the institution.

PHYSICAL ASPECT
Sports and physical activities conducted in schools help children to channelise their energy into something productive. It develops their physical as well as mental strength, and imparts various qualities like leadership, patience, teamwork, accountability, self-confidence, responsibility, and self-discipline. According to experts, such qualities if learnt at younger age, helps

HIGHLIGHTS

- School plays a major role in developing the thought process in kids
- School is the first avenue of socialising for a child. The place serves them the platform to befriend other children, and interactions with teachers and other staff help them to develop their social skills
- It develops physical as well as mental strength and abilities in students, and imparts various qualities like leadership, patience, teamwork, accountability, self-confidence, responsibility, and self-discipline

Why realists are happier than optimists

Positive thinking has long been extolled as the route to happiness, but a new study shows that realists enjoy a greater sense of long-term wellbeing than optimists.

For the findings, published in the Personality and Social Psychology Bulletin, the research team studied people's financial expectations in life and compared them to actual outcomes over an 18-year period.

"Optimists will see themselves as less susceptible to the risk of Covid-19 than others and are therefore less likely to take appropriate precautionary measures," said study co-author David de Meza from the London School of Economics and Political Science (LSE). "Realists take measured risks based on the scientific understanding of the disease," Meza added.

The findings are based on an analysis from the British Household Panel Survey — a major UK longitudinal survey — tracking 1,600 individuals annually over 18 years.

To investigate who among optimists, pessimists and realists have the highest long-term wellbeing, the researchers measured self-reported life satisfaction and psychological distress.

Alongside this, they measured the participants' finances and their tendency to have over or under-estimated them. They found that when it comes to the happiness stakes, overestimating outcomes were associated with lower wellbeing than setting realistic expectations. The findings point to the benefits of making decisions based on accurate, unbiased assessments.

"Plans based on inaccurate beliefs make for poor decisions and are bound to deliver worse outcomes than rational, realistic beliefs, leading to lower wellbeing for both optimists and pessimists," said study researcher Chris Dawson from the University of Bath in the UK.

According to the researchers, negative thinking should not replace positive thinking. Pessimists also fared badly compared to realists, undermining the view that low expectations limit disappointment and present a route to contentment.

"I think for many people, research that shows 'you don't have to spend your days striving to think positively' might come as a relief," said Dawson.

"We see that being realistic about your future and making sound decisions based on evidence can bring a sense of wellbeing, without having to immerse yourself in relentless positivity," Dawson added. IANS

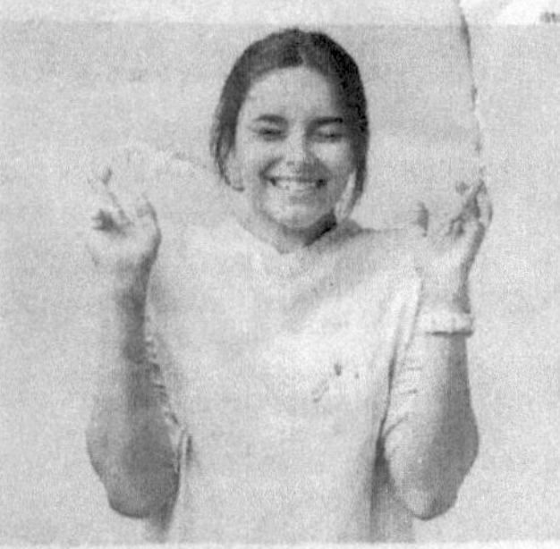

HAPPY-GO-UNLUCKY: Optimists are likely to make plans based on inaccurate beliefs, leading to worse outcomes

Convert Hard Times Into Opportunities

Gurudevshri Rakeshbhai

Do you feel you're passing through hard times? We may be facing a few health, financial, or relational problems, but more frequently, our hard times arise from our mind. Mental hard time is mostly a wounded ego. In such times, all we need is a shift in our thinking, the way we see and interpret life. Here are five tips to help us rise above challenges.

- Ask yourself, 'Is this the worst that can happen? How do you think you would have handled something worse than this?' It is our overthinking that makes any situation seem like it is hard to handle. The moment we change the track of our thinking to 'This is not the worst', the panic that crippled us subsides, and that situation becomes easy to manage.
- Instead of feeling bad, weak, blank or confused, let's think how we can utilise hard times to become braver, stronger, more creative and loving. You've been trying hard to achieve something but you are not successful. Think differently, 'If this doesn't seem to be yielding results, let me try another way.' We will discover within us, a surge of energy that will open up more avenues for handling the same situation efficiently and we will become braver and stronger.
- When you make a mistake, your wounded ego can blow it up to an extent that you condemn yourself: 'I am worthless.' Instead of being your enemy, be your friend. Be humble to accept your mistake and with a heart filled with deep gratitude and love, work hard to regain confidence. Turn a hysterical moment into a historical moment, one that you reminisce as an event that made you braver and stronger.
- Every day one cannot get sunshine. Learn to appreciate even cloudy weather. This will take away all your anxieties and insecurities. How can you be strong and creative if you keep complaining about life? All those you consider as heroes, even they have a lot of 'external sufferings'. When you learn to enjoy all seasons, you will become a bright and warm presence for those who need to rise above their clouds.
- Sometimes a bad day for your ego is a good day for the soul. We become more mature to endure and handle life passing through the fire of hard times. We always count our losses. Why don't we start counting our blessings? Sometimes we have to pay the price for our foolishness. But let's be grateful that we could catch at the bud stage before it could grow into a big disaster. In hard times, we get to know our strengths as well as our weaknesses. But knowing our weakness in itself is strength. Ultimately we come out stronger, wiser than before.

When life is showing us opportunities, we are busy planning ahead in time. 'Once this finishes I shall do this. And if this doesn't work, what would I do?' – not realising that life has already given solutions to all our problems, we are so busy thinking, that we miss the important lessons life wants us to learn. Make hard time a satsang. Understand that it is your desire and ego that is projecting difficulties. Don't just jot these points down. Repeat and apply again and again till they become your beliefs.

THE SPEAKING TREE

Education Through New Age Technologies

Technology is a game-changer for Indian education, which has tailored teaching techniques for better learning outcomes, writes Anand Dani

Technology plays a pivotal role in education, as it ushers in achieving significant improvements in both the teaching and learning process. Today, there are innovative techniques that combine classrooms with digital learning tools that help in increasing the student's engagement through a personalised learning approach. Artificial intelligence (AI) and machine learning (ML) have become an integral part of the teaching process that enable the student to learn with understanding. Educators are increasingly using technologies such as AI, ML, augmented reality (AR), virtual reality (VR) and gamification to increase the level of interest in the students and ensure maximum retention.

Virtual teaching assistants

AI and ML have enabled various learning capabilities such as digital classrooms, cloud-based content, e-books, virtual facilitators, interactive learning platforms and online assessments. AI-based learning solutions are dynamic and data-driven, which lead to an increase in prospects for better engagement among students. The technology can be used to develop adaptive learning methodologies through personalisation, identification and improve learning gaps specific to each student. AI will enable students to have virtual mentors and teaching assistants, which gives the teacher an added support system and keeps the student engaged at all times.

Engaging for students with gamification

Gamification in learning helps to keep the student's interest level high and captures their attention through game-like simulations and learning platforms. The idea of moving from one level to another keeps the student engaged and helps teachers know their progress. Understanding the weaknesses of the student, they can modify the process of teaching.

Going beyond imagination with VR

These technologies have helped students through interactive-learning approach with animations, images, videos and similar other content. These digital tools help to create an immersive environment for the students, which they can interact with and are much more experiential with a two-dimensional way of presenting the learning material than traditional pedagogy by reading topics in textbooks. This is helpful, especially in subjects such as science wherein the topic discussed in the classroom is showcased through animation or immersive simulations with AR and VR.

Technology is a game-changer for Indian education, which has tailored the teaching process for better learning outcomes.

(The author is chief business officer, Educational Initiatives)

How AI Is Making Education Interesting And Better For Students

Artificial intelligence (AI) has been playing an important role in every field, including the education sector. AI-based platforms have helped students and teachers in getting a better learning experience. Most students find these quite interesting, exciting, and engaging. This article covers some common AI-based solutions in education and advantages of AI in the Indian education system

Sani Theo

Passing the English language test by a machine demonstrates the success and power of artificial intelligence (AI). When a machine learns things through machine learning (ML) algorithms and gives correct results, it is remarkable. As per a report from *newscientist.com*, an AI passed the English language test and achieved its best-ever scores. The result was a breakthrough and an interesting development in AI technology.

Another breakthrough was the AI-based program AlphaGo defeating humans in the complex board game Go held in South Korea in 2016. AlphaGo makes its moves based on knowledge previously learned through ML techniques.

AI has been playing an important role in every field, including the education sector. There are so many interesting things happening around AI technology in the education industry. This includes AI-based online classes, enabling personalised learning, helping students get

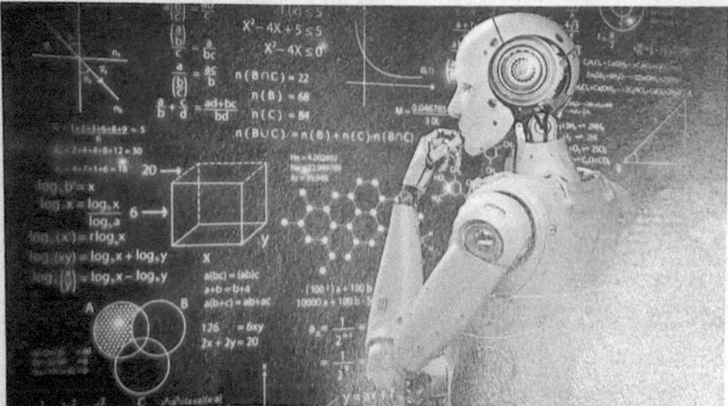

Representation of artificial intelligence (Credit: https://parentology.com)

better scores, etc. But what about teachers? What benefits do teachers get from AI technology? Will AI replace teachers in the near future? Before answering all these questions, let's first go through some facts about AI and its implications in the education industry.

This article covers some common AI-based solutions in education, use cases of AI-based learning platforms, and advantages of AI in the Indian education system.

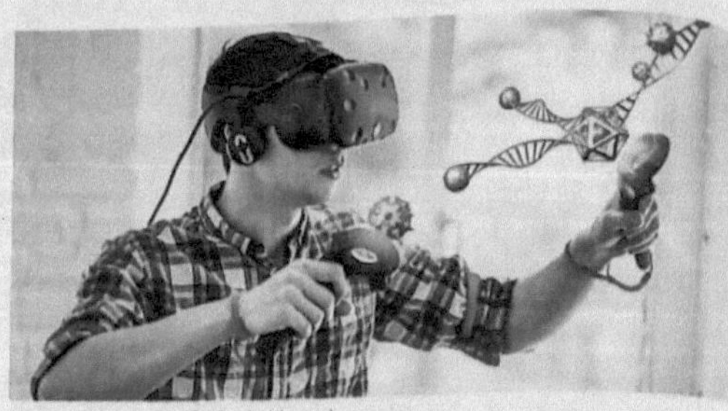

Virtual reality in education (Credit: xd.adobe.com)

AI-based solutions in education

There are many AI-based solutions available in the education field. There are great solutions available for school and college students. AI-based applications can analyse enormous amount of information and offer various options for students, including personalised learning materials.

Personalised learning. This is among the most important applications of AI that allows focusing on the individual needs of the student. There are firms like Dale Carnegie Training that offer many personalised courses. Through the use of AI technology, it is possible to create individual instructions, testing, and feedback.

Voice assistants. Some AI-based voice assistants available in the market include Amazon Alexa, Apple Siri, and Google Home. These gadgets are already in use for teaching and learning. Students can interact with these gadgets and get help without a human teacher. Since such AI-based assistants are new, most students find these quite interesting, exciting, and more engaging.

Smart content. This includes various learning materials, such as digitised textbooks, personalised contents, and customised interfaces.

Global learning. With AI technology, students can study various courses and get training programmes available in different parts of the world by sitting at home. There are many platforms with interactive learning materials available from the best tutors across the globe. AI also provides opportunities for students who speak different languages or have visual or hearing problems. There is an AI-based translator solution that creates subtitles in real-time mode. Using AI-based speech recognition, students can listen in their native languages.

Online classroom. Due to the outbreak of coronavirus, online classes have become popular than ever across the globe. A lot of companies have launched online classroom apps where students and teachers can interact through live video streaming, screen sharing, media-interactive presentations, etc. The most common online classroom apps used in schools include Zoom, Microsoft Teams, and Google Meet. Zoom has rolled out AI-powered transcripts, note-taking features, facial recognition, and more. Microsoft Teams is another videoconferencing app with a rich set of AI-enabled capabilities. Google Meet is a popular app with AI-based noise cancellation for video calls.

Eyeball tracker. This tool tracks learners' eye gaze and provides real-time feedback on their gaze patterns during lectures. The main goal is to investigate the attention patterns of students in the classroom and create a better understanding of their interests. It also aims to generate new insights into effective teaching techniques and keep students engaged during lectures.

Emotion recognition. Some schools have equipped several classrooms with cameras to recognise emotions of students. The systems automatically take attendance and track the activities of students, including reading, writing, or listening. Emotion recognition uses images rather than text as inputs. The images could be static photos of students' faces taken in real time. Using the system, the school can observe the behaviour of each student and take actions accordingly.

Virtual reality (VR). VR with AI provides outstanding visualisations that are not possible in traditional classrooms. The VR system uses immersive 3D visualisation technology to improve education and experiences. For example, when a student uses VR to understand the human heart, he/she will be able to visualise the whole system, including internal elements, pumping of blood back and forth inside the heart, and other functions. It helps in a better understanding of the concept.

AI-based learning platforms

There are many AI-based learning platforms already available across the globe. Some features of these platforms include the ability to analyse the knowledge level of a learner, offer backward communication, provide a plan for improvements, among others.

Beable. It is an integrated system launched by Achieve3000. It is a remote learning solution for middle school and high school in the US. It combines with data science, automation, and AI to deliver a tailored and multi-dimensional solution for students.

Little Dragon. It employs behavioural and emotional aspects of learning. An emotional AI detects states like boredom and frustration and then adjusts content to optimise the experience of learning.

Brainly. It is an AI-based solution offering personalised materials. It is basically a social learning community to help students. They can discuss issues related to their homework or gain new knowledge from other students. This platform utilises ML to provide a better user experience and assists in identifying spam and inappropriate content.

Doing housework may lead to sharper memory, better leg strength: Study

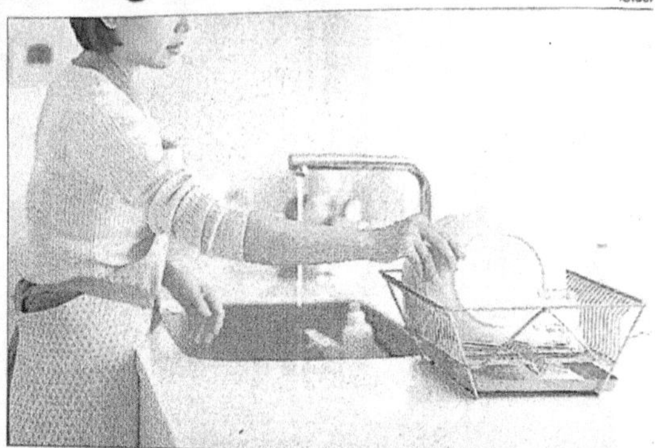

iStock

A new study has found that older adults who do housework may have a sharper memory, attention span, better leg strength and greater protection against falls.

Regular physical activity is good for maintaining optimal physical and mental health. And among older adults, it curbs the risks of long term conditions, falls, immobility, dependency and more. Yet global monitoring data indicates that in 2016, physical activity was well below recommended weekly levels and had budged little in a decade, with people in high-income countries more than twice as likely to be couch potatoes as those in low-income countries.

Given that housework involves physical activity and is an indicator of the ability to live independently, the researchers wanted to explore whether doing household chores might contribute to healthy ageing and boost physical and mental capacity among older adults in a wealthy country. They included 489 randomly selected adults, aged between 21 and 90, with fewer than five underlying conditions and no cognitive issues.

Participants were divided into two age bands: 21-64-year-olds (249; average age 44), classified as 'younger'; and 65-90-year-olds (240; average age 75), classified as 'older'. Walking (gait) speed and sit-to-stand speed from a chair (indicative of leg strength) were used to assess physical ability. Validated tests were used to assess mental agility and physiological factors linked to falls. Participants were quizzed about the intensity and frequency of household chores they regularly did, as well as how many other types of physical activity they engaged in. Light housework included washing up, dusting, making the bed, ironing, cooking, etc. Heavy housework included window cleaning, vacuuming, washing the floor, painting, etc.

The overall results showed that housework was associated with sharper mental abilities and better physical capacity, but only among the older age group. Cognitive scores were 8 per cent and 5 per cent higher, respectively, i those doing high volumes of light c heavy housework compared with those i the low volume groups.

Heavy housework was associated wit a 14 per cent higher attention score whi light housework was associated with : per cent and 8 per cent higher short ar delayed memory scores, respectivel Similarly, sit-to-stand time and balance coordination scores were 8 per cent ar 23 per cent faster, respectively, in the hig volume group than they were in the lo volume group.

— A

Lockdown Learnings: The Bhagwad Gita

Ami Patel

Bhagwad Gita Jayanti on December 25 held special significance for me, coming as it did in the ninth month of a series of lockdowns brought on by the pandemic. My mother and I enrolled in the 90-day-long Gita Swadhdyay classes. Waking up at 5.30am everyday and sitting through the class was in itself an achievement for a person like me, with very little attention span. Swadhayay is not just a lecture but also something that you listen to, and allow it to play and settle in your mind, and then make it a part of your life. Which is what I found intellectually challenging. It was conducted by Sanskrit scholar and former physics professor Swami Suryapad from the Art of Living, who elucidated the verses and the sequence with so much head and heart.

From the six chapters that Swamiji completed, there were some powerful shlokas whose meaning one could unravel for years. The ones that stayed with me the most were on the concept of yajna in chapter 3. Yajna is cosmic order rather than sacrifice, he said. The result of everything that happens to you or through you is the work and role of so many stakeholders. He gave us the simple example of the sugarcane juice machine where every part, from the nuts, bolts and wheels, to the handle that churns the machine are all important. Then how is it possible for one part to stake claim for the final outcome? That is why you have no right over the fruit of your action.

THE SPEAKING TREE

Play your role in life just like the sun, wind and rain; they don't expect a 'thank you' and just do what they have to do. Every person who comes into your life, every meal, every act, even your own breath, are all outcomes of yajna. So the honour, respect and gratitude for everything in creation arise.

Krishna reveals in chapter 6, the nuances of meditation and techniques to help one go deeper in the practice. In verse 5 he says, "Let a man raise himself by himself, not debase himself for he is one's best friend or enemy." I've always been big on self-effort and through the Art of Living courses I learnt that taking responsibility for your actions is key to success in life. No one in life can help you if you can't help yourself. With every action, thought and intention, you can choose to either raise yourself or go lower. However hard it may seem at some moments in life, in the end, it's only you. No spouse, friend or parent can do this for you and it's an illusion to think otherwise. This verse taught me self-reliance and discrimination, vital for personal growth.

"Treat victory and defeat, gain and loss, pleasure and pain alike and get ready for battle. Fighting thus, you will not incur sin," said Krishna to Arjuna (2:38). Gurudev Sri Sri Ravi Shankar says, "You are always a winner. Sometimes you win; sometimes you make others win." When you see the world and your experiences through this lens, opposites will not drag you down but keep your mind uplifted, no matter what! This was my gain during the Covid-19 lockdown – something that would never have happened in my schedule otherwise. Maybe work was slow but this gain was invaluable!

The writer, a celebrity fashion stylist, is also faculty, Art of Living

Education Is Alive When It Teaches Life Itself

Osho

Socrates once said, "I am like a midwife. I will bring out what is hidden in you." This is a tremendously apt definition of education. Fortune and misfortune are both hidden in man: nectar and poison exist in him: God and the animal both dwell in him. And this gives man the glorious freedom to choose whatever it is he wishes to become. The right kind of education will be the one that shows him the path to godliness.

But it must be remembered that when a man does not strive towards the achievement of a better life, he automatically sinks to a level even lower than that of the animal. The fact that a man has been born is enough to achieve this kind of fall. It is always easy to slide down; it requires work and constant application of oneself to rise. It takes effort, courage, determination. Rising upwards is an art, the greatest art in life.

The aim of an authentic education must be to teach this art, to teach the art of becoming one with God. The goal of education must be life itself, not merely providing instruction in how to earn a livelihood. In itself this means nothing. It is often mistaken as the aim of education ... The means of a man's livelihood is only the existence of his body, and education will only be alive when it teaches life itself.

THE SPEAKING TREE

To teach life is to teach knowledge of the self. A man may know everything else, but if he is unaware of the existence of his self then all of his knowledge is negated. Of what use is knowledge that does not have the self as its centre? The illumination of the whole world is useless if the self is in darkness.

To begin this ascent to consciousness, the first step must be in the direction of self-knowledge. The extent to which a man begins to know himself is the extent to which his animality declines.

The perfection of self-knowledge establishes a man in God. Only in that attainment is there fulfilment.

Each man carries the seed of that supreme development, of that ultimate perfection within him, and unless those seeds are fertilised, he will remain barren. His situation is not unlike that of seeds sown in the earth. Only when they are watered and cultivated do they sprout; only then do they poke through the soil and reach the light of the sun. And the sense of anxiousness, the feeling of restlessness that exists between the sowing and the harvest is an excellent sign, because only after restlessness can there be peace. And education can intensify, sharpen this wonderful time of restlessness in young people.

When education moves towards real knowledge and real peace, a new man and a new humanity will be born. Our future depends on this. The fate of mankind is in the hands of education. If man is to be saved from himself, it is essential that he be reshaped and re-created. If this does not happen, the animal in man will destroy him. The only escape from this nightmare is for mankind to establish itself in God. (Abridged from Immortal Words, courtesy: Osho International Foundation, www.osho.com)

Learn, Engage, Play

Digital game-based learning is proving to be both, fun and life-changing. Millions of children are engaging with smart technologies for education

Bijin.Jose@timesgroup.com

Learning and classrooms have transformed radically in the last few decades. In 2020, after the pandemic, education has taken a new dimension with schools shifting from traditional classrooms to virtual classrooms. Gone are the days when parents expressed apprehension over technology and digital gaming. Today, they and their wards are embracing digital game-based learning.

Virtual learning seems to be a game-changer with the brisk progress in digital game-based learning technology. Owing to access to technology, learning has become fun through digital games. This has altered how students learn. While mobile gaming has been a fascination among the youth around the world for years, however, they serve an entirely different cause today.

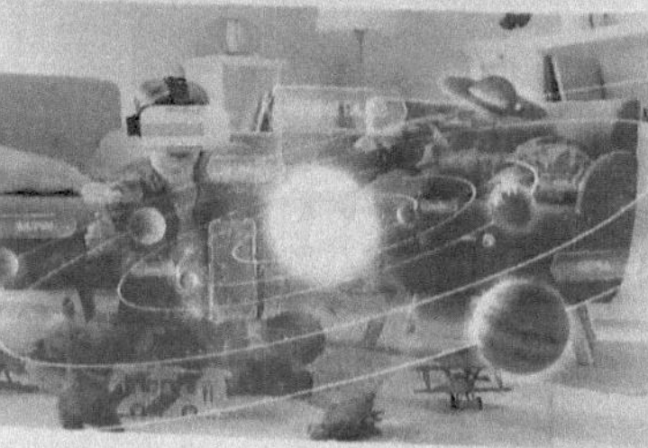

In 2021, as we read, programs are being developed to assist humans in various ways. Today, there is a gamut of applications and programs that are aiding education worldwide. Following the pandemic and the subsequent lockdowns, one thing that kept many connected and informed was the smartphone. From healthcare to education, shopping to delivering groceries - smartphones came as a saviour. Indeed, in the education sector, smartphones and smart technologies quickly adapted to the change and made waves with their digital classrooms.

Digital game-based learning applications are also acting as an effective medium to enable students and enhance their learning abilities. These applications are subverting the stigma associated with online gaming that has been often associated with just play and no work. Digital gaming applications have evolved over the years.

ALL ABOUT ATTENTION

The definition of gaming is no longer restricted to casual entertainment, they have extended to various learning games that have proven benefits. Most of these applications work on memory retention, word memory, and divided attention.

Each of our actions is driven by goals and we are often bound by endless options and forced to prioritise. This prioritising needs focus and memory. Attention and working memory support the best extraction and retention of information for optimal task performance. Hence, it is one of the first developing cognitive skills. Several studies show that early childhood attention skills correlate with long-term academic performance as well as acute and long-term behavioural issues.

DIGITAL GAME-BASED LEARNING PROGRAMS HELP STUDENTS STAY INTERESTED AND FOCUSED IN WHAT THEY ARE LEARNING. ENGAGEMENT WITH GAME-BASED LEARNING LEADS TO STUDENTS HAVING MORE MOTIVATION TO ACCOMPLISH TASKS

Today, over 136 million children struggle with attention deficit symptoms. However, technology is equipping them with the right tools to improve attentional performance, assess, and detect inattention. It has already been established, through various studies, that playing games can improve cognitive development like greater sensitivity to contrasts, sharp memory, and superior eye-to-hand coordination. However, with the new league of innovators and digital games, the process of learning has been accelerated, making them more accessible and manageable for both children and teachers.

TECH VS TRADITIONS

The new-age digital game-based learning applications are scalable as they assess attentional capabilities and detect difficulties with attention during early childhood. They mostly consist of cognitive tasks that assess the performance of children and offer meticulous reports.

Digital game-based learning has proven to be more effective in improving specific areas like students' mathematical learning than compared to traditional methods of learning. Since most games are interactive and rooted in math, young students have embraced this tech-enabled gaming.

According to experts, students are getting more engaged with the contents offered on these digital games. The dynamic content strike a balance between classroom lessons and virtual educational gameplay. Another set of experts believe that classrooms that use both traditional lessons and digital game-based learning have the most positive effect on students. Game-based learning offers affective, behavioural, cognitive, and social engagements to students.

INCREASING SCREEN TIME

According to the Ericsson Mobility Report 2020, the daily average screen time of Indians have been increased by an additional two hours. This shift took place due to work-from-home, virtual classrooms, entertainment and streaming services that witnessed a surge owing to lockdowns.

The screen usage on smartphones increased to as much as five hours, and when connected through broadband (Wi-Fi), the screen usage moved up from 2.5 hours to 4.5 hours. Last year, India witnessed a near 20 per cent surge in overall online consumption. As many as 77 per cent of parents admitted that information and communications technology helped them continue with the education of their children at home.

The recent trends in technology make game-based learning the best alternative to traditional learning methods.

CONSUMER CONNECT INITIATIVE

Technology cannot replace the teacher in the class, but it is reshaping education for our children's future

TECH FOR PURPOSE

THE CHANGING PEDAGOGY OF CLASSROOM EDUCATION

Technology should come in classrooms, but it is important that we intregrate technology with curriculum. I suggest NCERT to move towards technology and see how it enhances education and learning experience

MANISH SIDODIA
Deputy Chief Minister, Delhi

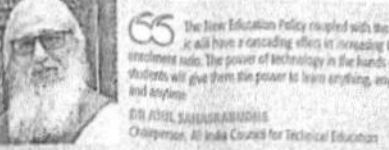

The New Education Policy coupled with the pandemic will have a cascading effect in increasing the gross enrolment ratio. The power of technology in the hands of the students will give them the power to learn anything, anywhere and anytime

DR ANIL SAHASRABUDHE
Chairperson, All India Council for Technical Education

Arsh.Shanbaug@timesgroup.com

In the last two years, technology introduction has changed the way classrooms are transected and how students are evaluated.
As students are returning back to their classrooms, schools must carefully consider the long-term role of technology and must adept technology with their class curriculum.

LEVERAGING TECHNOLOGY FOR QUALITY EDUCATION

Manish Sisodia, Deputy Chief Minister, Delhi stated that the development of the education sector cannot be achieved without technology. "The pandemic has been a blessing in disguise for the education sector because schools were forced to use technology," he said.

International standards of education accommodate local needs and atmosphere and there was a need to decode the needs of the Indian schools.

"Technology will help us achieve a holistic development of our students," Sisodia explained.

Sumeet Mehta, co-founder and chief executive officer, LEAD stated that School EdTech can truly empower teachers and can help them with the tools and methods to teach well.

"It can enable principals and school administrators to run their schools as world class institutions, and for the child it can open up access to learning beyond their local resources," he informed.

CONCEPT OF SCHOOLS STILL IMPORTANT

Former Education Secretary in the Government of India, Winda Sarup opined that though technology is a great enabler, the concept of physical school is needed to help the child grow. "There are social values like sharing, equality or honesty or even skills, like dance, music or art, a child learns only in the school atmosphere," she explained.

Sarup elaborated that technology introduction has changed the old pedagogy of the classrooms, "Even in a government school, technology has zoomed in the classroom and it is equipping the students with the world learning. EdTech will only enhance the child's ability," she added.

IMPACT OF SMART PHONES

Narayan Ramaswamy, National Leader- Education and Skill Development, KPMG India explained that one of the reasons parents prefer to send students to school rather than opting for home schooling is to ensure the child's social development.

"If in a village, students from schools suddenly become a part of a much larger world, it would help them in the medium to long term. But now in the short term, we are using the digital only world and using it as a substitute for what we have," he said explain that it has resulted in students becoming inward driven.

Due to the pandemic, schools were forced to experiment and learnt the use of technology to impart education. Due to which the education using technology and internet has become the order of the day.

Dr Anil Sahasrabudhe, Chairperson, All India Council for Technical Education stated that the usage of EdTech as an artificial intelligence based personalised learning platform is helping students.

"In a classroom where all students are sitting together, you would not be able to address to the needs of every child. It is here where technology is an enabler," Dr Sahasrabudhe said.

He informed that looking at where the student is, the technology program will take him on a journey which is shorter or longer, depending on the child's ability.

By making digital technology available to a much wider audience and making it multi-dimensional, either through blended learning or through artificial intelligence to augment it, EdTech is going to be a game changer for the education sector in the future.

Teachers are now beginning to leverage technology to reach out to students in a way that could only have been imagined earlier.

Technology can augment and enhance a school's role in a student's life, but we are in a social set up where we learn and grow, that's the idea of a composite school

VRINDA SARUP
Former Education Secretary
Government of India

What is heartening that the National Education Policy 2020 talks about an extensive use of technology in teaching and learning, in removing language barriers and also using digital technology to education planning, management and administration

NARAYAN RAMASWAMY
National Leader- Education and Skill Development, KPMG India

We need Tech For Purpose that delivers learning outcomes and prepares students for life, not just for exams

SUMEET MEHTA
Co-founder and Chief Executive Officer, LEAD

Key to success? Reconnect with your work every day

Getting into the right mindset for work can set the tone for the rest of your day — and it's especially beneficial for managers, a new study has found.

As per the study, published in the *Journal of Vocational Behavior*, mentally reconnecting to work — thinking about what you want to accomplish that day, what's on your day's agenda or what situations you want to encounter — can better prepare employees to be engaged throughout the day.

Pic: Getty Images

On days when managers and leaders were able to do this, they reported higher positive moods and work focus, which allowed them to be more successful.

The study's lead author Charlotte Fritz said they focused more on leaders because they are also responsible for the work and engagement of their employees. "Leaders' behaviour is crucial for a variety of employee outcomes," Fritz said. "(Such as) Providing a vision, being inspirational and motivating for employees, listening carefully and supporting employee needs and providing them with opportunities for growth."

— ANI

Pic: Getty Images

VARIETY
SATURDAY 18 DECEMBER 2021

5 important life skills to teach your kids

Pics: iStock

Have you ever questioned if your child is self-sufficient? Will your child be able to look after himself if you leave them alone for a long time? Do you believe your child possesses the required life skills to face the challenges that lie ahead?

As parents, we always wish to inculcate in our children certain characteristics. When we consider certain basic attributes, we find that leadership is one of the most important skills that any parent wishes to instil in their child. However, as parents, we must recognise that independence and confidence are the pillars of leadership. So, let's look at some very fundamental new learning skills for kids that will allow them confront the world on their own and with confidence.

Your child's education must go beyond what he or she learns in school. In order to learn, a child must be taught at home through experiences and training exercises.

MONEY MANAGEMENT AND BASIC BUDGETING

Among life skills, this is a very basic one. Every week or every two weeks, give your children a set amount of pocket money to use for their costs. Ask them to save up their pocket money if they want to buy something more expensive. They will be more motivated as a result of this. Comparative purchasing, falls under the umbrella of budgeting education. Open a bank account for your child and have them deposit money into it once a month (money received as gifts). Saving and valuing money will be instilled as a result.

MANAGING TIME

You're most likely perplexed as to how this is possible. You can accomplish this by encouraging your child to take charge of their own time. Instead of you waking them up, get them an alarm clock so they can get ready for school on time. Get them a planner to keep track of schoolwork and extracurricular activities, as well as when things need to be completed.

ABILITY TO MAKE DECISIONS

Education, jobs, and life partners are just a few of the major decisions we must make in our lives. How about teaching your child how to make good decisions from a young age? Here's how you do it: you teach kids how to make sensible judgments in short, straightforward steps. Begin by asking them to pick between two distinct activities or games, two different forms of clothing, two different foods, and so on. When this occurs, the youngster will be able to comprehend the repercussions of each, helping them assess the benefits and drawbacks!

THE IMPORTANCE OF ENVIRONMENTAL PRESERVATION

Instilling the value of environmental preservation and sustainability in your child at a young age will encourage them to be more caring for the environment. Make simple lifestyle changes at home to teach your child why environmental protection is important. Encourage children to be environmentally conscious in everything they do. You can even compel them to participate in environmental activities such as gardening and rubbish collection for disposal. Give them a section of your yard to plant whatever they like, if you have one. Assist them in sowing seeds and assign them the job of watering the plants. You can always use planting pots if you don't have access to a yard.

RESILIENCE AND ADAPTABILITY

These skills can be accomplished by ensuring that you do not constantly provide solutions to your child. Empower your child to solve problems on their own so that they are prepared to handle problems as they arise. They must develop resilience in order to adapt to a variety of circumstances and settings.

Make sure you have an open line of communication with your child so you can understand what they're going through and assist them. Teaching our children life skills is essential so that they know what they want to accomplish with their lives and, more crucially, recall the type of person they want to be. Focus your efforts on educating children in a fun and engaging way so that they may be confident in their values and talents! IANS

How to grow through failure

It is the responsibility of parents to teach their children that the road to success is paved in failure, writes Aachal Jain

Everywhere we look, other people's achievements loom large, whether it is the perfect happy families we seem to be surrounded by or the success stories detailed on social media. Society pushes us to paint a perfect picture of achievements and success to gain respect and value. It forces us to fear failure and settle for a life of mediocrity.

As individuals, we all know that failure is inevitable. We know that the path to success is paved in failure. There are so many stories that highlight failure as a stepping stone to success like those of Edison, Walt Disney, Steve Jobs, and many more. They constantly remind us that with every failure we have the power and ability to learn more and learn better.

Role of parents

It stirs panic when parents realise that their children are battling failure. We feel the need to rescue our child's self-esteem, by stepping over their hurdles and making everything 'perfect' and 'better'. As failure is painful and it causes emotional turmoil and distress, and inflicts agonising pangs of guilt, regret, and remorse. But in our efforts to protect them and in turn ourselves, we end up taking away from them a valuable opportunity of learning from their mistakes, stepping out of their comfort zone, being vulnerable, and most importantly, managing challenging feelings.

Several famous people in history have spoken about the lessons taught by failure. They had ideas that they put into motion when they were rejected. They failed many times, but each time they redirected their energy differently in achieving their goals. They had a growth mindset, which allowed them to believe that they have not achieved their purpose just yet. In the words of Walt Disney, 'We don't look backwards for very long. We keep moving forward, opening up new doors, and doing new things, because we are curious and curiosity keeps leading us down new paths.' Here are four things you can do to G.R.O.W. from those moments when you perform less than your best:

Growth Mindset

Failing at something allows you to dive deeper, reflect, and develop new perspectives. It forces us to start operating from inside our strength zone but outside of our comfort zone. It emphasises the power of 'yet' and is based on the idea that our brain is malleable and can be moulded to learn new skills.

Resilience

Failure allows us to develop resilience – the ability to bounce back. A study at The Kellogg School of Management, Northwestern University, states that trying again to accomplish our goals only works if you learn from your previous failures. The idea is to work smart, not necessarily hard.

Opportunities

Failures open the door to new opportunities. It allows us to learn, to grow, to become better, and to improve our skills. Revaluate the reasons for the setback, listen to others' feedback, analyse the situation, and apply your finding for the next opportunity.

(The author is a psychologist and Pastoral Care Coordinator, Aditya Birla World Academy)

ISTOCK

Sharmaji ka beta is learning to code but does your kid need to?

FOMO is driving parents to enroll their children in pricey coding classes but these are not a magic wand that will turn Junior into the next Zuckerberg

Ketaki.Desai@timesgroup.com

Jitendra Ramchandani was skeptical about introducing his daughter to coding. As a UI/UX designer, he has been straddling the tech and design world for the last 15 years, and the last thing he wanted to do was to stunt her creativity. "Design helps people use their brain more creatively while code instructs your brain to follow step-by-step instructions. My wife and I had been guiding my daughter in designing, making sketches and objects so her thinking is more outbound. But when she turned nine, we introduced her to coding," says the Jaipur resident. His daughter has been enjoying her coding course for the last three months but Ramchandani says he has doubts about the ...l promises being made to parents. "I recently got a certificate that said: Congratulations, your daughter is the youngest game designer and has learnt deep UI and UX. As a UI/UX professional, I ask how can you ... the word 'deep' around? They're making a fool out of parents."

CODING MANIA: While coding helps children learn computational and problem solving skills, the focus on grades and certificates may put too much pressure on young kids

> **What this kind of aggressive messaging does is make parents, who are in any case trying to find what's best for their kids, feel that teaching young kids to code is the only way out**
>
> — PARUL OHRI | Momspresso

Over the last few years, parents and kids are being bombarded with messaging that ... coding as a must-have skill for the ... Nothing too wrong with that except ... many such courses have poorly ... teachers, cost a lot of money and ... an unrealistic picture of little crore-... programmers.

...shek Singh Bisht, an IT professional and YouTuber who makes content about coding and technology, says that while he agrees the demand for coding will be on the up and up in the future, the rush and pressure with which parents are making their kids code is problematic. "Programming can be an elementary skill, like how you teach kids the fundamentals of maths and science. But the way it's being portrayed is putting too much pressure on kids to perform. They're teaching them software development without teaching them fundamentals of computer science, like how a computer does what it does," says the 23-year-old Bengaluru resident.

Prateek Shukla, CEO and co-founder of Masai School, which is an online academy that teaches software development for students of class 12 onwards, says there is undue pressure on kids because everyone has FOMO (fear of missing out) and is scared their kid will be left behind. "The 'Sharma ji ka beta syndrome' is everywhere. That should not be the objective. Programming is essential to develop computational thinking, but not every child is so inclined and there is no point in forcing them."

While the skills involved in coding, such as problem solving and computational thinking, are important for children, Parul Ohri, chief editor of parenting platform Momspresso says the level of introduction to coding that schools are doing should be enough, particularly in the coming days since the New Education Policy has announced that coding will be introduced to students in class six onwards. "What this kind of aggressive messaging does is make parents, who are in any case trying to find what's best for their kids, feel that teaching young kids to code is the only way out," says Ohri.

Like much else in India, it has become a way for parents to show off, Ohri says. "Are you telling children that if you make an app, your life is made? Look at the number of startups that fail."

These days one doesn't even need to know coding to make an app with tools like No Code. No Code creates a similar result as coding, but instead of having to write lines of code, you can drag and drop to create the app or website you're looking for. Some argue that this is a way for kids to learn a simpler way of doing things, without having to go knee deep in programming. Karthi Subbaraman, an educator and co-founder of Noco Loco, an online school that teaches No Code, says that while it may be easier for kids to pick up, she still would not recommend that they learn it.

As a mother of a 16 and 12-year-old, she has never made any attempts to teach them coding. "Your prefrontal cortex is still developing till you're 20. That's why we're stupid in our teenage years and can forgive easily." She adds, "I am thinking of creating a design thinking course for children to teach them how to think creatively. If a kid comes to me and says I want to create an app to sell my sandwiches, I would tell them first sell some sandwiches, then let's think about making an app."

Divyansh, a 21-year-old product engineer at a startup, says he started coding three years ago and is quite passionate about it. But he admits that while it is very rewarding, it is not always fun and can be somewhat exasperating. The Gurgaon resident says, "Coding comes with some consequences that I can cope with as an adult. The stress, looking at a screen for 5-6 hours, the feeling of frustration when you have a bug and can't figure out why something has failed — it could be a nightmare for a kid."

Shukla says that instead of certificates and set courses, coding for kids should be more fun and gamified, like code.org which makes kids feel they're not learning when they are.

The value of this approach is echoed by 28-year-old Rishabh Srivastava, who runs loki.ai, an artificial intelligence startup. He says, "In Europe, most of the US and Canada, it is essentially STEM toys that are used. But in India, China, Japan, Singapore and South Korea, the focus is on certification courses where kids can be graded. That takes the fun out of it."

As for more coding jobs, perhaps that is inevitable with automation but it also implies demand for jobs that cannot be automated, he points out. Srivastava says, "Jobs that require great human connection will also become a lot more popular."

A tuition teacher who plays PS4?

Companies Are Roping In Young, Tech Savvy Graduates To Help Kids Learn Lessons, Finish Homework And Ace Tests Outside School

Kamini.Mathai@timesgroup.com

Tanveer Singh Sethi, a Class X student, recently found himself a 'productivity friend'; someone to help him navigate his school curriculum, work with him on acing his tests and getting him prepared for his impending board exam. All this, while also listening to music with him, DJing and talking about basketball.

"It doesn't feel like tuition or school," says Tanveer, who paired with his study friend through the site Mentor Match. "It's more like a friend helping me study. We use flashcards, YouTube, and write down keywords, and in between, talk about things that interest me, like DJing," says the student of Sishya School. "It makes studying more interactive."

Started by friends Rohit Raheja and Sachit Dugar during the lockdown, Chennai-based Mentor Match connects college students or recent graduates with school students from classes III to XII to help them study.

"We match students and mentors according to interests," says Rohit, an architecture graduate. "So, if it is a Class IX football-loving IIT aspirant, we match him to an IIT student who also likes the game. We find that it helps keep the child motivated. Our study buddies are young; they are on Instagram and would be happy to play a round of PS4 with the kids. It's all about building a rapport to make studying fun."

Sachit explains that the mentors are not like tutors or school teachers who focus more on teaching the curriculum. "We help a student study the lessons, and ensure they are revised and ready for their exams." They now

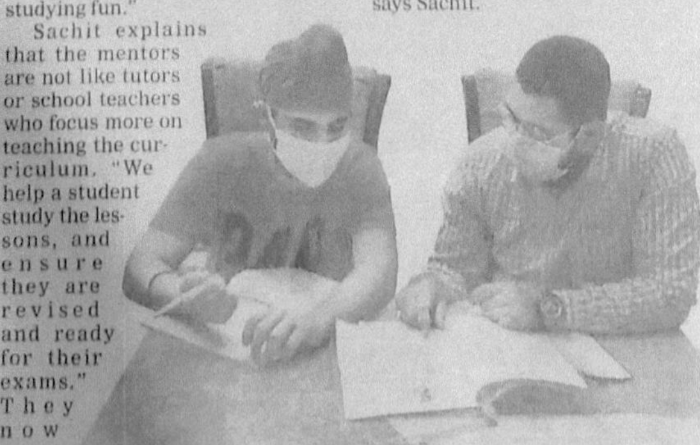

work with 400 mentors from different colleges. "The concept of doorstep tutor buddies has caught on during the pandemic when classes have gone online and students are left on their own to learn the lessons. For mentors, it's a great part-time gig," he says.

Another Chennai-based organization, Thejomaya, run by Uma Yogesh, promises 'homework buddies' for children up to Class V, where they are guided to study as well as complete their homework. "For Class VI and above, we offer proctoring services on a subscription-based model," says Uma. "Here, students can log in at a certain time and ask their queries - whether specific to a homework problem or more generalized queries like how to set up a study timetable or to revise for a test. We work with students one-on-one and tailor answers to their specific questions."

Nandini Chopra of the Delhi-based startup MyStudyBuddy also offers help beyond the school curriculum. Their 'buddy at your doorstep' helps children "learn to learn". "We don't stick to what is in the textbook. If students, for instance, have a speech to give the next day, they can work on creating that speech, diction, etc with their study buddy," says Chopra.

"Most students know what to learn, but lose their way when it comes to how to study. Mentors and study buddies can help students find a smart, fast and efficient way to go about it. And that's a lesson for life," says Sachit.

Focus On Action

ANUP TANEJA

The *Bhagavad Gita* is a testimony to the painstaking efforts made by Ved Vyasa, collating material contained in the *Upanishads* and presenting to people a complete philosophy of life in a most convincing manner. In presenting this wonderful guide to life, the purpose was to share with the world the deep spiritual knowledge acquired through intense spiritual sadhana and by the grace of Krishna, and reveal to seekers the best way to attain Self-realisation — the ultimate beatitude.

ARUNOYUTI DAS

The 18 chapters of the *Gita* are all interconnected. In the first discourse, the *Gita* dwells on Arjuna's despondency which is assuaged in the second discourse wherein Krishna speaks of immortality of the soul.

Seeing Arjuna regain his stature and composure, Krishna says to him:

1) One should remain calm and unperturbed in both loss and gain, success and failure

2) Sin is born of ignorance and all acts done in a state of ignorance shall forge fresh chains of bondage

3) Attachment is of the essence of ignorance; eradicate attachment and you will be able to cut off ignorance

4) Only action is thy concern and not the fruit; forget all thought of fruit and fight. Indeed, in that detachment to fruit lies the secret of success! This eradication of the thought of fruit; this annihilation of the 'i-thought,' false ego; remaining calm and unaffected by success and failure, is yoga. Yoga also means performance of actions with dexterity. Here there is no laxity in making the right effort, no going back; even a little success achieved is considered highly creditable.

GITA JAYANTI

This *jnana* imparted by Krishna inspires Arjuna a great deal — so much so that he not only learns the technique of karma yoga and renunciation of the fruits of actions but also further succeeds in restraining his turbulent senses through the practice of concentration and meditation.

Seeing Arjuna make good progress on the path of spirituality, Krishna then imparts to him knowledge of his various *vibhutis*, manifestations, in order to prepare him for the vision of his *vishwarupa*, cosmic form. Arjuna then spontaneously understands the nature of a liberated soul and also of the field and the knower of the three gunas, qualities of nature. The knowledge acquired by Arjuna eradicates all his doubts one by one. Thus, going step by step up the ladder of yoga, Arjuna ultimately sets foot on the highest rung of the spiritual ladder wherein realisation dawns upon him that the entire universe is a blissful play of Consciousness. It is the sublime state where the mind merges in the Pure Self and the seeker becomes a *jnani*, a liberated soul.

In the words of Paramhansa Yogananda: "So comprehensive as a spiritual guide is the *Gita* that it is declared to be the essence of the ponderous four *Vedas*, 108 *Upanishads*, and the six systems of Hindu philosophy. Only by intuitive study and understanding of these tomes, or else by contacting cosmic consciousness can one fully comprehend the *Gita*. Indeed, the underlying essential truths of all great world scriptures can find common amity in the infinite wisdom of the *Gita's* mere 700 concise verses". ■

Gita Jayanti is being celebrated between December 24-26, 2020. Anup Taneja is author of 'Bhagavad Gita: Gandhi's Eternal Mother', IGNCA, 2020.

Why skill development must be the key to K-12 system

Empowered teachers who develop unique practices can create a system that produces exceptional minds, writes **Naman Jain**

The K-12 schools in India are among the biggest education systems in the world. With a student base that crosses millions and solid legislation that have ensured that access to schools is not a distant reality for any student, we have over the decades, succeeded in building a strong system that provides for a solid education. The advantage of a K-12 system is that there are predefined levels with assigned learning goals, which not only makes imparting education easy but also makes it easier to assess whether learning outcomes are being achieved or not.

Restricting original thinking

Despite the successes, there have also been shortcomings, particularly with respect to students' complaints that the system encourages rote learning. The examination system, too, is critiqued for encouraging memorisation and not encouraging original or innovative thinking. Thankfully, all this is set to change with the shift in narrative that focuses on bringing skill development to not just the curriculum but also to the pedagogies and examinations. Skill development is not just an area of focus for those in higher education or those seeking employability; instead, it is a necessary overhaul that must be integrated with the K-12 system, too. The discussion in the media tends to frame skill development as a concept that is necessary to improve the fortunes of prospective job seekers. However, it must be a tool that can bridge the gaps, if any, in the learning system and offer the students a chance to add elements of novelty to their current education.

The teaching methods must focus on bringing real-life challenges to the classrooms

A successful education system is not defined by students' ability to get high marks alone. It is defined by its learning and instruction features, its curriculum and pedagogies as well as its ability in preparing students for the challenges of the future. The methods of teaching must focus on bringing real-world challenges to the classroom, enabling students to look beyond the narrow confines of their textbook while they learn to not just solve problems but even anticipate them.

Focus on areas of interests

Policymakers are aware of the need to incorporate real-life challenges in the curriculum and each time a revamp of the syllabus is done, it is done to make it contemporary and relevant. For instance, introducing project-based learning allows students to carve their niche by identifying their areas of interest and focusing on building something new based on what they have learned. It allows them the right amount of independence and freedom which is necessary for innovation and creativity while ensuring that they are aligned with the needs of the system.

SCHOOL GUIDE

Skills needed to face life's challenges

The purpose of any education, particularly a K-12-like system which sets the foundation of one's learning journey is to impart new skills that prepare one for life's challenges. It is pertinent to remember that in this learning journey, books or exams are just means and not ends. The system must be inclusive in that it accounts for differences in learning styles as well as the efficacy of different teaching aids.

If teachers are empowered to develop their own practices that can help them enhance the existing skills while inculcating newer skills, we can create a system that produces exceptional minds with immense creativity and innovation. A good example would be the use of technology. We need to make students use motor skills, technical skills as well as intellectual skills, which are an important part of the pedagogical style.

When one hears the word skill development, the mind immediately goes to short-term, employability-friendly courses. But the point here is to notice that the focus on skill development goes beyond courses to include a shift in pedagogies and curriculum. It reflects an educator's understanding that the skills of the future will be new-age and difficult to predict. Hence, the education that we impart today must be built on a strong base so that it can withstand the challenges of the future.

(The author is education policy expert, and director (Development), [illegible])

Education 4.0 will transform the higher education landscape

Our institutions must become demonstrators for the conversion of knowledge to wealth by addressing the social problems, writes academic V Ramgopal Rao

India has seen tremendous growth in its higher education landscape since independence. From about 20 universities in 1950, we now have ıbout 1040 universities. About 135 ɔf these institutions are regarded ıs Institutions of National Impor:ance (INI). Close to 39 million stu:lents are currently enrolled in the ıcademic institutions with India's Gross Enrolment Ratio (GER) standing at 27.1%. Though the higher education system has scaled, there are often concerns expressed from multiple quarters about the quality and relevance of the education we impart to our students.

Progress in the higher education sector

1950-51

23 Number of universities

700 Number of teachers

0.174 **million** Number of students enrolled in higher education

0.7% Gross Enrolment Ratio

2019-20

1043 | Number of universities

15,03,156 | Number of teachers

3,85,36,359 | Number of students enrolled in higher education

27.1% | Gross Enrolment Ratio

Sources: Nehru Memorial Lecture by Sukhadeo Thorat, former chairman, UGC, University of Mumbai, 2006; AISHE 2020

Diverse faculty is important

The higher education system has evolved in the last 200 years to become similar to the industry, thanks to the changes brought about by the advent of new technologies. While industry 1.0 was about mechanisa:ion and steam power, the subse:juent generations have been ena:led by the discovery of electricity, omputers, and the internet respec:ively. Industry 4.0 optimises pro:uctivity, quality and cost savings. imilarly, in the pre-electricity era, ducation 1.0 was all about learning om a teacher. The teacher played a ntral role while the student was e recipient of knowledge. With e advent of electricity, computers and the internet, we have now moved to Education 4.0, where it is all about anytime, anywhere and on-demand learning. The role of the teacher has changed from being an instructor to that of a mentor, coach, and collaborator. For Education 4.0 implementation, the changes begin at the curriculum level. The curriculum requires the right mix of technical knowledge, social sciences, ethics, leadership skills, design elements and it also needs to be tightly integrated with out-of-class learning. Flexibility is the key and emphasis must shift to faculty, where IITs can play a role through the Quality Improvement programmes.

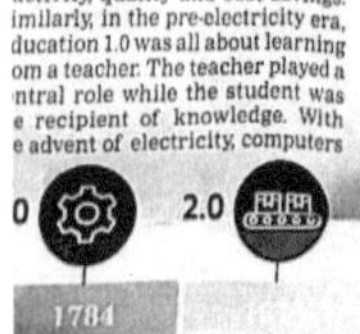

Innovation and idea factories

Many high-tech industries today spend enormous amounts of money internally to carry out research in advanced areas such as AI, Quantum computing, Robotics, etc. The leading players in such advanced areas are industry labs, not academic institutions anymore. This is done more to retain the IP and to gain a leadership position in these strategic areas. With industry research directly competing with academic research, the only way academic institutions can survive is by becoming idea factories. For this to happen, we need to encourage multidisciplinarity in our institutions. Innovation thrives when unlike minds come together.

There is also a need for the institutions to be locally engaged and globally networked. They need to become a demonstrator for the conversion of knowledge to wealth by addressing societal problems. A diversified financial model is important for the sustenance of institutions' growth. Some of our finest public-funded institutions in India, today earn as much as 1% to 7% of their revenue from tuition fee. While we do not want to burden our future generation of students with huge fees, we need to make them responsible through the 'Study now-Pay later' schemes, similar to the Australian Higher Education Loan Programmes (HELP). HELP scheme by Australia is different from a standard loan. In the HELP scheme, an individual commences repaying their loan only when their taxable income reaches a certain threshold.

(The author is Pillay Chair

Archaeology of transforming the learning landscape

Re-imagining and redesigning a forward-looking, flexible knowledge structure is a necessity for enabling youth to face an uncertain future, writes academic RP Tiwari

The accelerated pace of change in the 21st century compels India to embrace an education system that ensures life-long learning, ability to skill, upskill and reskill continuously and promotes out-of-box thinking, entrepreneurship, agility and enduring adaptability. Reimagining, reinventing, and redesigning a forward-looking, flexible education system is a necessity for making youth ready to face the challenges of an uncertain future. We need to break the barriers that exist between the education system and real-life situations. For this to happen, the focus of teaching should be on how to learn independently, reinvent oneself, understand real problems of society and the environment, and develop expertise to solve those problems. It is a well-settled fact that learning from books and the materials available on the virtual platform has no relevance unless it is supplemented with hands-on experiments, discussion/debate, quiz, project/internship/dissertation, field study, case study, interview, prototypes, and other forms of experiential learning.

Imparting holistic learning

Apart from the provisions of a multidisciplinary coherent curriculum designed for imparting holistic education, multiple-entry-multiple-exit (MEME) options, academic bank of credits (ABC), institutions with research and teaching centricity, multidisciplinary education and research universities, NEP also provides for pedagogical and evaluative reforms. Face-to-Face (F2F) pedagogy currently in vogue has not yielded tangible results, as is evident from the results of the several surveys conducted for assessing employability. Though F2F teaching has several inherent advantages, the striking deficiency is its inability to satisfy the diverse needs of learners.

For this reason alone, hybrid learning (HL) is fast emerging as the alternate pedagogical pathway for the new-age learners.

Hybrid learning is not merely a blending of offline and online mediums of instruction but a mixing of structural, disciplinary and pedagogical experiences as well at appropriate proportions. It helps personalise learning modules in terms of time, techniques and learning preferences. It facilitates a wide range of learning styles either in an offline or an online session facilitated by a teacher. The flipped classroom is one such session where students learn the lessons prior to attending F2F session. The teachers usually play the role of mentor to answer questions and facilitate discussion. Learners can watch activity-based videos, read digital material at their convenient time and pace and become better prepared for group work/discussion, debates, quizzes, hands-on practices, role- playing, projects, and case studies in the classroom environment. Flex learning, gamification, virtual labs and other self-directed learning styles help motivate learners to go deeper into a subject.

Since online learning material is designed as an alternative to in-person material and is meant to bring in flexibility, the curriculum for the hybrid learning environment must be different from that of the physical classroom. HL model facilitates personalised learning as it ensures a variety of synchronous and asynchronous learning activities aligned to learning styles.

Gradual and not abrupt switching over to hybrid learning will help learners and mentors

Pitfalls of HL

However, there are certain pitfalls of HL, like it can work best with the support of smart devices and high bandwidth stable internet connectivity. Selection of appropriate LMS and customisation of existing courses for HL through mapping of learning goals, needs, styles, and pace are the other issues. AI helps in the mapping of such attributes and eventually in customisation. We have an opportunity to convert 'digital divide' to a 'digital provide'. Since the ultimate purpose of embracing HL is to combine the strengths of traditional and online learning to ensure a higher degree of engaging learning experiences for the satisfaction of learners and mentors alike, HL should not be implemented just for the sake of it. Rather, it should be implemented in true spirit and intent to leverage maximum benefits.

(The author is Vice-Chancellor of Central University of Punjab, Bathinda)

No learning online

Physical classes have been suspended in schools in India for over 1.5 years now. While some students were able to study online, learning was inaccessible for most. Two surveys — School Children's Online and Offline Learning (SCHOOL) and Annual Status of Education Report (ASER) — evaluated the impact of the pandemic on learning. In August 2021, only 8% of children in rural areas and 25% of children in urban areas studied online regularly. Among them, many found it difficult to follow the curriculum and had connectivity issues. As a result, the % of children who could read and perform calculations declined from pre-pandemic levels

Hunting for network: Students attending online class at a reserve forest in the Niligiris in Tamil Nadu. • SATHYAMOORTHY M

1 In March 2021, ASER conducted a study in 24 rural districts of Karnataka to estimate the learning loss and understand the current status of learning. Nearly 18,000 children between the age group of 5 and 16 were assessed for their reading and arithmetic skills

2 The SCHOOL survey covered 1,362 underprivileged children in August this year across 15 States. It focused on children in rural hamlets and urban 'bastis' who generally attend govt. schools. About 60% of them resided in rural areas and nearly 60% belonged to Dalit and Adivasi communities

1. MANY NOT IN CLASS | Only 28% of rural children studied regularly while 37% didn't study at all. Of those who were able to study, only 8% regularly attended online classes or learned through videos

% OF CHILDREN WHO WERE STUDYING IN DIFFERENT WAYS IN AUGUST

	URBAN		RURAL	
Type	Regularly	Sometimes	Regularly	Sometimes
Online classes/ videos	25	16	8	8
Watched TV	3	5	0.1	1
Private tuitions	24	6	14	4
Studied at home (with family's help)	15	29	12	25
Studied at home (without help)	19	30	15	31
Studied with friends in each other's houses	2	13	3	11

% OF CHILDREN WHO	URBAN	RURAL
Studied regularly	47	28
Studied from time to time	34	35
Did not study at all	19	37

Educating children through television has not taken off despite regular educational broadcasts on Doordashan. Those who could afford private tuitions studied more regularly

2. LEARNING ROADBLOCKS | The major problems for children who didn't study online regularly were the lack of online material or the unavailability of a device. 43% of parents in rural areas said no online material was sent by the school, while 36% said their children did not have their own smartphone

Main reasons why children did not study online regularly in households that had a smartphone	URBAN	RURAL
Child did not have their own smartphone	30	36
Poor connectivity	9	9
No money for "data"	9	6
Online study was beyond child's understanding	12	10
No online material was being sent by the school	14	43
Other	15	10

EXPERIENCE AMONG CHILDREN WHO STUDIED ONLINE

% of children who studied online and...	URBAN	RURAL
Had their own smartphone	11	12
Watched live classes, not just videos	27	12
Had connectivity problems (often/ sometimes)	57	65
Found online classes/videos difficult to follow	46	43

Among those children who studied online, the majority of them said that they faced connectivity issues and found online classes difficult to follow

3. LEARNING LOSS | According to ASER, in rural Karnataka, the % of Class 5 students in govt. schools who could read Class 2-level texts decreased from 47.6% in 2018 to 32.8% in 2020. The basic arithmetic ability of such students also reduced

READING ABILITY

Year	% children in Class 5 who can read Class-2 level text		% children in Class 8 who can read Class-2 level text	
	Govt.	Pvt.	Govt.	Pvt.
2014	45.7	53.5	70.1	72.2
2016	41.9	42.8	69.7	71.2
2018	47.6	41.8	70.1	71.5
2020	32.8	25.5	66.8	65.1

ARITHMETIC ABILITY

Year	% children in Class 5 who can do at least subtraction		% children in Class 8 who can do division	
	Govt.	Pvt.	Govt.	Pvt.
2014	49.4	70.2	34.5	43.3
2016	54.6	68.7	39.9	49.2
2018	52.5	60.8	[illegible]	47.4
2020	41.5	50.4	30.6	46.2

www.ingramcontent.com/pod-product-compliance
Lightning Source LLC
LaVergne TN
LVHW041159150826
845673LV00001B/218

* 9 7 8 9 3 9 5 6 7 3 1 3 6 *